Colonial Gardens

COLONIAL GARDENS

Rudy F. Favretti
Gordon P. DeWolf

BARRE PUBLISHERS
Barre, Massachusetts: 1972

COPYRIGHT © 1972 BARRE PUBLISHERS

INTERNATIONAL STANDARD BOOK NUMBER 8271–7230–3
LIBRARY OF CONGRESS CATALOG NUMBER 75–185321

Acknowledgments are made to *Arnoldia*, the publication of the Arnold Arboretum of Harvard University, for material contained in this book.

PRINTED IN THE UNITED STATES OF AMERICA

ALL RIGHTS RESERVED

CONTENTS

The Design of Colonial Gardens	*9*
How to Create or Restore a Colonial Garden	*27*
Flowers before 1700	*37*
Herbs, Aromatic, Culinary, and Medicinal before 1700	*76*
Vegetables and field crops before 1700	*84*
Shrubs, Trees and Vines before 1700	*96*
Fruits and Nuts before 1700	*107*
Flowers, 1700 to 1776	*116*
Vegetables, 1700 to 1776	*121*
Shrubs, Trees and Vines, 1700 to 1776	*123*
Fruits and Nuts, 1700 to 1776	*141*
Appendix	*143*
Bibliography	*159*

Colonial Gardens

I The Design of Colonial Gardens

LANDSCAPE ARCHITECTS and horticulturists usually extend the colonial period 64 years to 1840. By including the years from 1620 to 1840 we can tell a more complete story even though the period isn't historically correct.

There are several reasons for this. Garden design changed little until about mid-point in the Greek Revival period. Then there was great change with the advent of Victorian architecture and styles.

One reason for such gradual evolution may have been the limited number of books published on the subject. Most of those available until after the Revolutionary War came from England or France. Few were published in the colonies. Similarly, there were few nurseries and seed houses until after the Revolution. Another reason may have been the preoccupation with protest against restrictive arts and with independence.

Actually gardens changed very little during this period, even in Europe. Except for the development of the so-called 'natural style' in the 1700's, garden design deviated very little from the Tudor style, even in England. By extending the colonial period to 1840, we are able to include the effects of the 'natural style' on the development of American gardens.

THE GARDENS OF EARLY PLYMOUTH PLANTATION AND RURAL NEW ENGLAND

The gardens of the Pilgrims were purely a functional outgrowth of their needs. The house and barn formed the focus and the site was divided into pens and barnyards near the barn, with the garden placed near the house. The orchard and fields were planted where soil and exposure seemed best but not always near the 'home lot.' The plot was studded with sheds, hayracks, coops and other necessary appurtenances.

The size of the garden was in proportion to that of the family. Most of the vegetables needed on a small scale were grown in the fenced-in garden near the house. These included leeks, onions, garlic, melons, English gourds, radishes, carrots, cabbages and artichokes. A variety of herbs were grown among the vegetables, the most aromatic grown to one side so as not to 'flavor the soil.' Vegetables needed in large quantities like maize, beans and pumpkins were grown in fields.

The herbs were used in cooking, medicines and for fragrance. A popular dish was a variety of vegetables stewed in a pot with meat and herbs. Herbs for medicine were harvested and dried for later use. The herbs for fragrance were hung in rooms, sprinkled among linens and clothing, or carried in a pocket.

Flowers were grown, too; some just to look at, but most for utilitarian purposes. Rose petals, for example, were dried for fragrance. If the lady of the house liked flowers, she often collected violets and mayflowers from the woods and transplanted them into her garden, for it was she who tended them. Otherwise, only those flowers needed for food, medicine, fragrance or dyes were grown.

There was no garden plan as such. In other words, no conscious effort was made to plan a garden in today's sense. The house and outbuildings were sited according to the topography, exposure and needed relationship. Areas related to them were fenced or penned and walkways through the gardens were laid down as direct routes from doorway to outbuilding or as seemed best for tending the plants.

The plants were planted in no particular order. Tall plants obscured short plants, flowers were mixed with vegetables, and among them all were herbs. Some of the vegetables may have been planted in blocks according to the European practice of the time. The beds were often raised by building up the soil and holding it in place by saplings laid on the ground. Great emphasis was placed on drainage.

The walks were usually tamped soil, sometimes gravel, and occasionally they were surfaced with crushed clam shells. These walks were just wide enough for a person to walk through the garden or weed one of the beds from it. The main walkway leading to an outbuilding may have been wider.

The walk and bed pattern was not necessarily symmetrical nor regularly patterned, as in the parterre gardens of the merchants in Boston. Instead, the walk pattern was often irregular and the beds varied in size and shape according to what was grown in them and how they fitted between the functional walks.

The gardens of the Dutch in New York, on the other hand, were often laid out on a highly symmetrical plan with perfectly balanced beds on either side of a central walkway with a series of balanced secondary walks throughout.

The Plymouth-type arrangement prevailed throughout the colonial period and well into the 19th century in agrarian New England. Numerous old farms laid out in the latter part of the 17th century and during the 18th century reflect this scheme with little variation.

One such plan was executed on the Nehemiah Williams Farm in Stonington, Connecticut. This farm was recently sold after having been in the same family, handed down from father to son, for nine generations. The plan remained essentially the same throughout that period. The buildings were sited to the northwest of the house to protect it from the prevailing winter winds. The orchard was so located to perform a similar function and to be handy to the house and sheds.

The gardens were not in one large block as we plant them today. The south garden, which was on a 3–5 per cent slope, was so placed to capture the warmth of the spring sun for early crops like peas, lettuce, radishes, carrots, beets and onions. The bean garden did not have a southern exposure but it was protected by two walls, out of the path of the northwest winds, so that the soil would warm up in time for bean planting which was later than lettuce and peas. This garden later became a flower garden.

The two gardens in the front lot were for later vegetables and second plantings of some of the early ones. Also fruits such as strawberries, currants, gooseberries and rhubarb were grown in the front lot garden next to the wall.

Flowers were grown in the dooryard garden to the front, or south of the house. This garden was in full view of the two front parlors or chambers, and people approaching these rooms on special occasions would have passed through them. Dooryard or parlor gardens were very popular in the 17th and 18th centuries, reaching the height of popularity after the Revolution.

Dooryard gardens were usually enclosed with wooden fences. These fences often started at the corners of the house and came straight forward. In the case of the Williams garden, the fence went to the stone wall. Where a similar house was close to the street, the fence would have gone to its edge.

This plan persisted well into the 19th century, as Fig. 1 and the cover indicate.

The Gardens of Merchants and Townsmen

In contrast, the merchants who lived in Boston, New York, Philadelphia or most other colonial cities and towns had gardens quite different from those of their brothers in the country. Their gardens were formal, laid out in a symmetrical pattern with each side of a central walkway reflecting the other. These gardens imitated the formal parterre with which many of the merchants were familiar in their homelands.

During the colonial era, great emphasis was placed on siting the house on a high piece of ground. Sometimes the foundation was purposely built high and the soil dug from the cellar was mounded around it to form a terrace or a series of them. Occasionally, additional soil was brought in to complete a particular terrace plan, but this was not often done. In fact, it is a characteristic of building in the colonial era to search for just the right, natural site for the house rather than to change the topography as we so often do today.

The garden was placed near the house so that the family could enjoy the view and the fragrance. Some writers of the time suggested an eastern or western slope for the garden in an attempt to benefit from the heat generated by the rays of the sun. Many suggested avoiding a southern slope because the sun would be too hot and the plants would 'hang their Heads, to wither away, and die' as John M. A. Lawrence writes in *A New System of Agriculture*. Other authors of garden books suggested a southern exposure to gain maximum benefit from the sun's rays.

Actually, we find that in northern climates gardens were often sited on a southerly slope, especially vegetable gardens for early crops. Flower gardens were ideally placed on level spots because it wasn't as important to force perennials into bloom and the annuals couldn't be planted until late in the spring. In other latitudes we find gardens at all exposures depending on the site and philosophy of the owner.

The gardens were usually enclosed. Rarely do we find records of a garden without a fence, wall or hedge around it. These enclosures were not only to lend privacy to the garden but also to protect it from the winds.

Walls were not used as extensively in America as they were in England, Holland and other European countries. Certainly they were important in some cities, especially in southern New England. But except for a few, it seems that most of the gardens in New England were enclosed by wooden fences or hedges. Perhaps they were heeding the advice of John Lawrence who wrote in 1776 that the sun and the wind were the worst enemies of plants and gardens. 'Walls are some defense, where they are tall and

FIG. 1: *A typical, rural plan showing the layout based on functional needs. Pen and ink, probably Massachusetts or Connecticut, artist unknown—1840.* Photo: courtesy of Old Sturbridge Village, Sturbridge, Massachusetts.

the garden little; but otherwise they occasion great Reverberations, Whilles, and Currents of wind, so they often do more harm than good. I should therefore choose to have the Flower Garden encompassed [sic] by hedges ... which after frequent clipping are not only more ornamental than the best of walls, but by far more useful, and better defences against the merciless Rage we are speaking of, both with Respect to the Flowers themselves or the female Lovers.'

In many communities we find early ordinances regulating the height of fences. Usually, a higher fence was allowed along the sides and back of the property with a lower one specified for across the front. The style and architecture of the fences were endless, ranging from the homely picket fence to a solid board fence with a slatted, louvered or latticed top.

The garden plan within the enclosure was a variation on a basic theme. It consisted of a central walk usually on axis with a door of the house. Secondary walks radiated from the central walk, sometimes at right angles and other times at acute angles. The central walk was terminated by some sort of feature and often some of the secondary walks were, also.

These terminal features might have been one or many. Summerhouses, arbors, specimen plants and gates were quite common, while statues, sundials and steps were also popular. Sometimes the focus was merely an opening in a fence, wall or hedge, framing a spectacular or pastoral vista.

The length of the garden, its central walk and the complexity of the secondary walks were in proportion to the extent of the owner's financial resources and his love of gardening.

On either side of the central walk and between the

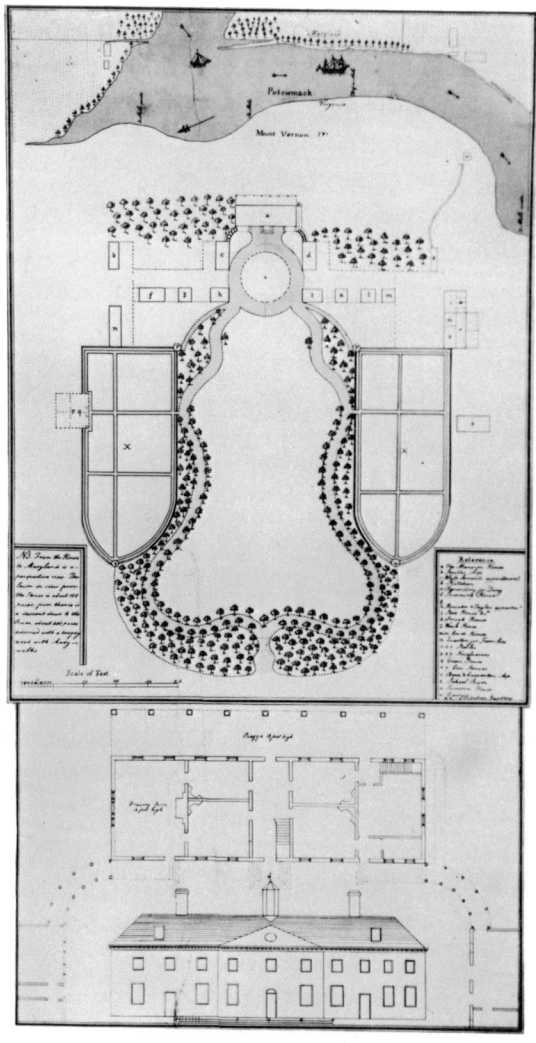

FIG. 2: *The VonGlummer reproduction of the original Vaughan plan of Mount Vernon. This plan shows the formal design of the Flower Garden (left) and the Kitchen Garden (right) on either side of the park-like bowling green and serpentine avenues surrounded by trees.* Photo: courtesy of the Mount Vernon Ladies Association of the Union, Mount Vernon, Virginia.

secondary paths were the flower or garden beds. Some were square; others were rectangular, triangular, or round, depending on the design of the secondary walk system. It was not at all unusual to find all of these forms within one garden, especially if it was a large one. According to Lawrence, the form would 'vary according to a Person's different Fancies; yet ought to throw the whole into Variety within Uniformity . . . but care must be taken to contrive it so that it may be easily seen, that the curious Artist may find Admittance to the Beds in every Part, either by the large or by lesser Gravel Walks or Paths; so as by the reach of the Arm every Operation may by performed with Ease.'

Lawrence goes on to say that oftentimes the wide central walk had one round bed in the center 'filled with some curious Ever-green plant cut pyramidically or fluited.' Sometimes there were a series of circular, triangular, square or rectangular beds down a very wide central walk.

Around the outside of the garden and just inside the enclosure there was often a large bed or border encircling the entire garden. One description of an early garden states that there were eight square beds in the center with two wide borders running along the fence, all tied together by a series of gravel walks between beds 'raised by boards.'

This typical pattern, used almost without exception, was imposed on every type of site, regardless of the topography. There are numerous descriptions, drawings and plans of colonial gardens where the central axis walk plan was imposed on a sloping site. Most of the gardens on old Pemberton Hill in Boston had this arrangement going uphill from the house, and the beds were on a series of terraces. Philadelphia had its classic examples, and one of the best garden examples using this arrangement is on the grounds of the Moffatt-Ladd House in Portsmouth, New Hampshire. This garden was restored according to an old record made by the Ladds who came to the house in 1819. It is unique for the set of grass steps which (combined with an arbor as background) is the focus for the central path.

The arrangement of plants within the garden varied with the whim of the owner. Sometimes the gardens we have described were devoted entirely to flowers. Others combined herbs with flowers. Mary Mathews Bray, in *My Grandmother's Garden and an Ancestral Orchard*, writes: 'In our garden, according to custom of the time, four beds (of eight) were given to herbs useful in cooking or for household remedies.' Some of the beds were even given over to vegetables, depending on whether or not the owner had a special kitchen or vegetable garden elsewhere on the property.

Fruit trees were often found in the garden and trees in general were included. Shrubs and roses were placed in the border beds that encircled the garden, but sometimes they were placed in the beds themselves as shown in Fig. 3.

There was no special massing of flowers and herbs for effect. Bray writes: 'In those days a garden was not usually arranged for the effect as a whole . . . each plant was cherished for itself, and was put where it seemed best for its individually, or often, of course, where it was most convenient . . . four corners of one bed were filled with fleur-de-lis (iris) white and blue . . . and the corners of another with Sweet Williams.' The taller flowers were often planted in the borders around the outside, but sometimes they were planted in the center of the beds with shorter plants surrounding them.

The massing of plants and the repetition of these masses

FIG. 3: *This companion 1792 painting of Mount Vernon, East Front, shows the barely visible forms of deer (foreground) and the fence built to confine them.* Photo: courtesy of the Mount Vernon Ladies Association of the Union, Mount Vernon, Virginia.

to give continuity of design was not a 17th- and 18th-century principle of garden planning. Gardens during that period were tied together by the system of walks, beds edged with boxwood, ribbon grass, moss pink, pinks (*Dianthus*), lavender (*Santolina*) and germander, or by the enclosure around the whole garden.

Today some think of the colonial garden plan as intricate and involved to no real purpose, but as we study it we find that it was a logical outgrowth of the times. The involved walk system was laid down to divide tall flowers from short flowers, culinary herbs from flowers, and medicinal herbs from vegetables. These walks made the beds accessible for cultivation, admiration and harvesting. As many walks are needed, they felt, why not arrange them in an interesting pattern? It was necessary to fence the garden, for privacy and also for protection against the wind and marauding animals. The fence provided a suitable site for tall plants, giving them background and interest, and the plants softened the harsh outline of fence or wall. A practical as well as attractive solution.

What about herb gardens? Some 20th-century gardeners think of colonial gardens only in terms of herbs, probably because herbs are so popular in culinary art today and we are generally familiar with them. But during the colonial period, unless one was engaged in the growing of herbs for sale, as the Shakers and some others were, most people did not have a separate garden for them. These plants, as previously mentioned, were grown among the flowers and vegetables or in a part of the kitchen garden.

Country Estates on the Outskirts of Town

The gardens described were laid out on the smaller, tighter sites along the streets of cities and towns. This does not imply that all city lots were small, for some were of several acres. But they were often narrow and the parterre plan lent itself well to this shape of lot. Even people of limited financial resources used a similar but smaller version of either the Plymouth type or (more often) the parterre type of garden plan.

In the early 18th century, Joseph Addison, Alexander Pope and Sir Richard Steele wrote satire about the rigid, formal garden filled with topiary and enclosed by a wall. Dorothy Stroud, in *Capability Brown*, tells us that Addison revised his own planting to 'run into as great a wilderness as their natures will permit.' Bridgeman, a leading landscape architect of the period, was greatly influenced by their satire, banishing sculpture and elaborate design in favor of bits of woodland in the landscape. William Kent became famous by eliminating walled enclosures and substituting ha-ha walls to separate areas inconspicuously.

This so-called 'natural style' was carried to its heights by Lancelot 'Capability' Brown and others in the 18th century. In fact, Brown's gardens are often characterized as 'a round lake, an open lawn, and a copse of trees.' This influence was felt in the colonies by the wealthy plantation and estate owners. By the late 1700's, most wealthy properties covering vast acreage, whether in Virginia, Philadelphia, along the Hudson River, or in New England, were designed or 'layed out in the natural style.'

New England was, on the whole, most conservative with this style, probably because the various functions necessary to run the household were housed under one roof because of climate, rather than strung out as at Mt. Vernon, Monticello and other southern estates. For this reason, an arrangement of buildings pulled close together lent itself better to the formal plan than to the 'natural style.'

New England was not without its 'natural' gardens, however. Numerous estates surrounding Boston, for example, were laid out in this manner, and Samuel McIntyre suggested such a plan for the Elias Haskett Derby Mansion in Salem, Massachusetts. Theodore Lyman's 'Waltham House,' purchased in 1795, 'arranged the grounds with ... noble trees, lake, gardens, terraces, lawns and a deer park.'

In fact, at least one garden in New England was revamped according to the style of the day. Miss Susan Quincy, in her *Memoirs*, tells how President Quincy changed the plan on the Quincy Estate, 'being a great lover of nature. Obstructions to views were removed; walls and fences leveled; lawns with trees and shrubs judiciously disposed, replaced the court-yard and gardens; and the approach to the house turned through an avenue of elms, a third of a mile in length.'

Mount Vernon is one of the best authentic examples of an estate that combined both the 'natural style' and the parterre plan (see Fig. 2). Approaching the Mansion is the Serpentine Avenue encircling the bowling green. Note how the avenue is heavily planted with trees (see also Fig. 3). Some of the original trees are still growing along this approach.

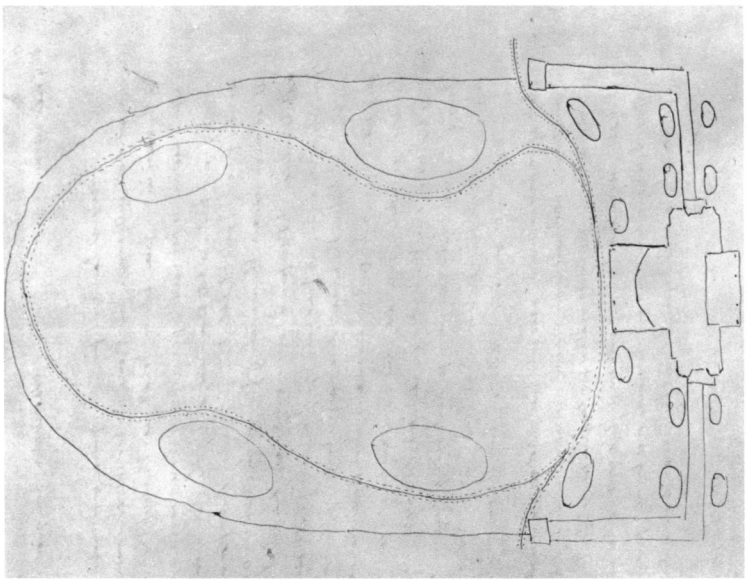

FIG. 4: *Thomas Jefferson's plan of the "Round-about Walk," flower borders (dotted lines) and beds (circles). The flower beds were laid out and planted in 1807 and the winding walk and flower borders in 1808.* Courtesy of the Thomas Jefferson Memorial Foundation.

On either side of the tree-lined avenue and bowling green are the parterred flower and kitchen gardens, both the same size and shape, differing only in detailed interior arrangement. Actually, the whole plan approaching the Mansion is symmetrical in design, though informally planted.

Between the Mansion and the Potomac River, however, is a broad expanse of lawn, a ha-ha wall (see upper right of plan in Fig. 2) and a copse of trees on the east front of the Mansion (see Fig. 3). This illustration shows that George Washington even included a 'Deer Park,' like so many of the estates in England. Washington wrote in 1792, 'I have about a dozen deer (some of which are the common sort) which are no longer confined in the Paddock which was made for them but range in all my woods and often pass my exterior fence.' Several early gardens in this country had deer parks, among them the 'Waltham House,' Estate of Theodore Lyman and the Robinson Estate, built in 1750, opposite the present West Point Academy on the Hudson River. Deer in the landscape made these seats more 'natural.'

Thomas Jefferson's plan also gets away from the formal, parterre layout, but it, too, is symmetrical immediately in front of the house (see Figs. 4 and 5). His plan has an informal walkway which he called the 'Round-about', and it was bounded by flower borders. These have been restored according to his plan (see Fig. 5). Near the house are circular beds which were planted in 1807.

The plan for 'Solitude,' the seat of John Penn in the Philadelphia area, shows an arrangement that would have pleased William Kent and Capability Brown. On this estate were a ha-ha wall, irregular flower gardens, a vista south of the house and a clump of trees to the east.

Along the Hudson River there were many estates

FIG. 5: *The restored flower beds and borders at Monticello as they look today.* Photo: courtesy of the Thomas Jefferson Memorial Foundation.

(Philipse Manor, Van Cortlandt Manor, and the estates of the Livingstons and the Van Rensselaers, among others) landscaped in the 'natural style' and less symmetrical than Mount Vernon, probably because of the more varied topography, but still with the parterre garden near the formal Mansion House.

Conclusion

It is safe to say that the gardens of the colonial period were planned according to the way of life of the owners. In rural agricultural areas the gardens were of the Plymouth type, laid out between functional walks and paths, but not as rigidly formal in pattern as the parterres of the city merchants, tradesmen and professionals.

When the influence of the natural style, carried to its height by Capability Brown, reached this continent, the owners of the large estates and plantations were affected by it but they retained the formal parterre plan for gardens near the house.

On the smaller city sites that did not lend themselves to the development of lakes, copses of trees and expanses of lawns laid out to imitate nature, the rigid parterre plan remained until well into the 19th century.

II How to Create or Restore
a Colonial Garden

IN HISTORIC PRESERVATION, the creation or restoration of early gardens should be a subject of major concern. Often the grounds and gardens are overlooked, but fortunately this is becoming less true as the century advances.

For many it is hard to know what type of garden plan to use, where to put the garden, how to enclose it, how large it should be, whether to include vegetables and herbs as well as flowers, and how to go about laying it out. It is best to hire professional assistance in the person of a landscape architect who is sympathetic towards the area of historic preservation and restoration. But sometimes funds do not permit this type of consultation and an individual or committee is appointed to develop the plans.

Naturally, the first thing to do is to research the site, the people who lived there and the records. Leave no stone unturned because the more you can find, the better and more individualistic the garden will be.

It matters not what area you research first. Let us start with the people who lived in the house: what they did; when they did it. If there were several families, find data on each and determine which one or which period you will represent. An example of this is the research that went into the garden the author designed for the Noah Webster House. Naturally we knew about the famous linguist, but he didn't live there after he became famous. So the obvious question was: what did his parents do? They were farmers, not wealthy, but of moderate means. The architecture of the house was simple, not elegant, suggesting that the garden should be small and simple and not contain unusual plants such as a vast array of tulips that had to be imported. Instead, the garden should contain plants needed for everyday sustenance.

Sometimes in researching the people who live in a house, you find facts that pertain directly to gardens. The garden at the Salem Towne House at Old Sturbridge Village contains many fruit trees because Mr. Towne experimented with fruit and actually developed a new variety of apple called the 'Porter.' These details lend interest and individuality to a garden.

Written and published records could shed much light on the gardens of a particular site. Probate inventories often mention orchards, walls and gardens, and some have been known to have plans attached. Some probate records name fruit trees by variety. But even if the inventories or wills contain no mention of gardens, they give you an idea of the relative standing of the person. This is invaluable information because it offers guidelines concerning a size for the garden and the elegance of the proposed plan.

Deeds can offer garden information. The author recently came across one deed that mentions 'the southwest corner of the garden west of the dwelling house' as the

Garden of the Standish House at Plimouth Plantation with Pot Marigold, cabbage, carrots, red kidney beans, watermelons and muskmelons. Photo: courtesy of Plimouth Plantation.

beginning of a boundary. Upon investigating the site, the exact dimensions of the garden were determined with relative ease.

Diaries, journals, letters and personal documents usually contain a wealth of information. One has only to read the diaries of George Washington and Thomas Jefferson to get a clear picture of gardening and agriculture. Lesser known men and women kept records, too, on such facts as when flowers came into bloom, when seeds were planted, and how and when walks were laid. Account books, while they contain only facts and figures, are invaluable because in them are such items as listings of seeds bought, crops harvested, tools purchased, and materials bought to combine with herbs for household remedies.

Personal letters written from husband to wife, sister to sister, brother to brother, reveal much because it was the custom of the day to speak of plants in bloom in the garden, the change of season and its effect on the garden, what was harvested, and much more.

Town histories sometimes have descriptions of a garden or a site, but quite often contain sketches of houses showing their gardens and fences. It was in Caulkins' *History of Norwich, Connecticut* that we learned about some ordinances controlling the height of fences during the colonial period. John Warner Barber wrote 'Historical Collections of Every Town . . .' on many states in the early 19th century. His engravings of each town show gardens in some cases, fence styles, street tree arrangements, and many other details.

News articles and advertisements are helpful, especially in developing a list of plants. Many state and local historical societies have collections of early newspapers and broadsides. Articles sometimes appear commemorating a particular individual and sometimes his house and grounds are mentioned. Old essays, speeches, and pamphlets are invaluable. The archives of horticultural societies are full of this type of information.

The author relies heavily on paintings for information on the design of gardens. These works often suggest a fence style or garden arrangement typical of a particular town or region. We are aware of some murals that show village scenes that can be identified and many of these illustrate gardens.

One is not often lucky enough to find a plan. How many people make a plan today? Not many. The same was true in early times and many of the plans that were made have been lost. But do not overlook this aspect of research; sometimes the files of historical societies contain them. Even if it is not the plan of the site in question, if it is in the same region or area, you might get some ideas.

While word of mouth is not considered as reliable a source as the written word, you should consider it. On asking a member of the ninth generation of the Nehemiah Williams family if there ever had been a garden in front of the old house and, if there were, had it been fenced as most of them had been, he responded in the affirmative. Upon probing the site, we found the stub of a stone fence post that had broken off, proving that there was a fence there.

Probing the site itself often reveals much information. It is good to do this late in the fall when the tall grass has died down or early in the spring before it starts to grow. Then you can see the lay of the land. Sometimes you will find the remains of an old walk, and depressions on either side will suggest that there were beds there. Sometimes there are mounds instead of depressions, suggesting that the beds were raised.

Areas enclosed by walls or plants suggest that the enclosure was either a pen or a garden of some sort. One walled enclosure we found, family tradition says, was a children's play yard laid out to confine toddlers so they wouldn't stray into the woods.

An odd arrangement of trees or shrubs, having no meaning today, with careful study might suggest a garden plan. Large shrubs and small trees around the outside of an area with a depressed or raised spot in the central portion most certainly suggest a garden.

Sometimes removing soil from these depressed or raised areas or from around walls or house foundations will bring plants to life. Many times seeds that haven't been planted in years will germinate because they have been preserved in the depths of the soil. These may not necessarily date to the colonial period, but they may suggest how a present-day garden evolved.

Should There Be a Garden?

Sometimes there were no flower gardens because only vegetable gardens were planted, and flowers and herbs needed for food, fragrance and medicine were grown among them. Maybe there were a few flowers by the front door and some herbs by the kitchen, and that is all. This is where research about the people who occupied a given house may cast light on whether or not there should be a garden and what type.

If you are thinking of a garden for your own home, there are two ways to approach the problem. If you are a purist and want things just as they were then, proceed as suggested. But if you do not really like to garden and

Garden of the Winslow House at Plimouth Plantation, Plymouth, Mass. Pumpkins in foreground. Photo: courtesy of Plimouth Plantation.

cannot afford to hire a gardener, then perhaps just some fruit trees surrounding the property, some shade trees along the road, some lilacs at the corner of the house and near the shed, and some herbs by the back door will suffice, preserving the character of the site and yet not creating a burden on you.

If you have reproduced a site, or even if you have an old one and are not a purist, why not plan as our forefathers did, basing the plan on function: a dooryard garden near the front door to create an interesting entrance space, some trees to provide shade and define the front yard, some herbs by the back door and a little lawn for recreation, with a vegetable garden (if you want one) to the rear. This will satisfy your needs and, after all, that's how they planned in the colonial era.

Colonial Garden Plants

I Flowers before 1700

THE FOLLOWING plants are listed according to the names most commonly used during the colonial period. The botanical name follows for accurate identification. The common name was listed first because many of the people using these lists will have access to or be familiar with that name rather than the botanical name.

The botanical names are according to Bailey's *Hortus Second* and *The Standard Cyclopedia of Horticulture*. They are not the botanical names used during the colonial period for many of them have changed drastically.

We have been very cautious in interpreting names to see that accuracy is maintained. By using several references spanning almost two hundred years, we were able to interpret accurately the names of certain plants. For example, in the earliest works, Lark's Heel is used for Larkspur, also Delphinium. Then in later works the name Larkspur appears with the former in parenthesis. Similarly, the name 'Emanies' appears frequently in the earliest books. Finally, in 1665, John Rea, in *Flora: Seu de florum cultura*, lists the name Anemones as a synonym.

Some of the names are amusing: 'Issop' for Hyssop, 'Pumpions' for Pumpkins, 'Mushmillions' for Muskmellons, 'Isquouterquashes' for Squashes, 'Cowslips' for Primroses, 'Daffadown dillies' for Daffodils.

Other names are confusing. Bachelors Button was the name used for *Gomphrena globosa*, not for *Centaurea cyanis* as we use it today. Similarly, in the earliest literature, 'Marygold' was used for Calendula. Later we begin to see 'Pot Marygold' and 'Calendula' for Calendula, and 'Marygold' is reserved for Marigolds. The name 'Cowslips' for Primroses can be confusing for in some parts of the world that is the name used for 'Marsh Marigolds,' *Caltha palustris*.

'Winterberry' was a name commonly used for Chinese Lanterns (a modern common name), and 'Alkekengi' was also used for this plant. But one must be careful in reviewing the literature because *Ilex verticillata* and *Ilex glabra* might also be called Winterberry. 'Gilliflowers' is a name used for Dianthus and Stock, but there was also an apple by this name.

In parts of Virginia, the name 'Ivy' is used in reference to Mountain Laurel, *Kalmia latifolia*. Jefferson used the name 'Puckoon' to refer to Bloodroot, or *Sanguinaria canadensis*. In some parts of Connecticut, the name 'Ox-eye Daisy' was and is used for Black-eyed Susan, *Rudbeckia hirta*, but in most places 'Ox-eye Daisy' refers to *Chrysanthemum leucanthemum*. In a village within a town in Connecticut, Daylilies (*Hemerocallis fulva*) are called Wash-House Lilies, not Daylilies.

Unfortunately these common names were used freely, perhaps more so than the botanical names, such as they were. For this reason, the 'unraveling' of lists in old books and the compilation and documentation of new lists becomes necessary.

Wherever possible we have worked from primary sources. Where these were not available, we have used reliable secondary sources. A Bibliography of sources is included at the end of this section.

These lists have not been presented as complete and final compilations. We consider that an entire lifetime could be devoted to documenting the plants of the colonial period and then the list would not be complete.

The reader should be aware that most of the early gardeners who kept notes or wrote books were either wealthy or experimenters in the field of horticulture. For this reason, many of the species that seem unusual today were probably unusual then and for that reason should be used with restraint. Also, other plants may not have been used freely. Barberry, which was once commonly grown, was outlawed in Massachusetts in 1754 because it was suspected as an alternate host for wheat rust. Furthermore, plants such as *Kalmia latifolia,* Mountain Laurel, were detested by farmers because they were poisonous to livestock.

Some readers will be disappointed that varieties of fruits and vegetables are not listed. This was not within the scope of this article. Such listings may be found in numerous books on garden and fruit culture, one early one being *McMahon's Garden Calendar* by Bernard McMahon, published in Philadelphia in 1806. For the period this book had a large printing and is available in most horticultural libraries. The Worcester County Horticultural Society also has a list of available varieties from their experimental orchard.

WINTER ACONITE *Eranthus hymalis* (L.) Salisb.
Native of Italy, Silesia and Switzerland. Cultivated in England in 1596 by Gerarde. Desired for its yellow flowers in early spring.

ACONITUM, WOLFSBANE *Aconitum napellus* L.
Native of Germany, France and Switzerland. Cultivated in England in 1596 by Gerarde. Cultivated for its showy blue-purple flowers and the medicinal properties of its poisonous roots.

ALKEKENGI, WINTERBERRY *Physalis alkekengi* L.
Native from southern Europe to Japan, but now adventive or naturalized in many parts of the world. Cultivated in England at least by 1597. Originally grown for the fruits which were used medicinally. More recently the fruits with their inflated orange calyces have been used in winter bouquets.

AMARANTHUS, FLOWER GENTLE, *Amaranthus tricolor* L.
    JOSEPH'S COAT, TRICOLOR
Found throughout the tropics, probably native in Asia. Cultivated by Gerarde in 1596. Philip Miller, in *The Gardener's Dictionary*, wrote: 'The chiefest beauty of this plant consisteth in the leaves and not in the flowers; for they are small tufts growing all along the stalk, . . . every leaf is to be seen parted into green, red and yellow, very orient and fresh.'

    AMARANTHUS, GREAT FLOWER *Amaranthus caudatus* L.
    GENTLE, LOVE-LIES-BLEEDING
Native in the tropics. Cultivated by James Sutherland in 1683. John Parkinson, in *Theatrum Botanicum . . .*, wrote that 'the flowers stand at the toppes of the stalke and branches more spread at the bottome into sundry parts, the middle being longest, and usually when it is in the perfection hanging down like a tassell . . . of a more excellent scarlet red colour.'

ANEMONE, WINDFLOWER, *Anemone coronaria* L.
    EMANIES *Anemone hortensis* L.
Native of southern Europe and the Mediterranean region.

Cultivated in England in 1596, according to Gerarde, for their showy flowers.

ARMERIA, SWEET JOHN, *Dianthus barbatus* L.
SWEET WILLIAM
Native in Europe and Asia, south to the Pyrennees. Cultivated by Gerarde in 1596. Miller wrote that 'the common Sweet William . . . has long been cultivated in the Gardens for Ornament, of which there are now great Varieties which differ in the Form and Colour of their Flowers, as also in the Size and Shape of their Leaves; those which have narrow Leaves were formerly titled Sweet Johns by the Gardeners, and those with broad Leaves were called Sweet Williams.'

ASPHODELL *Asphodelus albus* Miller
 Asphodeline luteus L.
Both are native of the Mediterranean region and were known to Parkinson in 1640.

ASTER, STARWORT *Aster tradescantii* L.
 Aster amellus L.
Aster tradescantii L. is a North American plant cultivated by the younger Tradescant as early as 1656. *Aster amellus* L. is native in southern Europe and Asia. Cultivated by Gerarde in 1596.

BACHELOR'S BUTTON *Gomphrena globosa* L.
 Centaurea cyanus L.
According to Miller this name was applied to *Gomphrena globosa*. 'by the Inhabitants of America,' and *Centaurea cyanus* 'is called Bachelor's Buttons in Yorkshire & Derbyshire, but this name is given to many other flowers,' as, for example, double flowered forms of *Achillea ptarmica* L.

BALSAM *Impatiens balsamina* L.
Native in Southeast Asia. Parkinson grew it by 1629 from seeds sent from Italy, and Gerarde had it in 1596. Miller said that 'the Japanese use the juice prepared with alum, for dyeing their nails red.' There is also a European species with small

Bellflower, *Campanula*. From Parkinson, *Paradisi in sole*.

flowers which was early confused with our native *Impatiens capensis* Meurburgh.

BEARE'S EARS   See PRIMROSE

BELLFLOWER, THE GREAT   *Campanula pyramidalis* L.
  STEEPLE, OR CHIMNEY BELLFLOWER
Native of Southern Europe. Cultivated by Gerarde in 1596. 'This plant is cultivated to adorn Halls and to place before the Chimnies in the Summer.' Miller.
  PEACH-LEAVED BELLFLOWER   *Campanula persicifolia* L.
Native of Eurasia. Cultivated by Gerarde in 1596. 'Of this there are the following varieties, *viz.* the single blue, and white Flower, which have been long here; the double Flower of both Colours, which have not been more than twenty Years in England, but have been propagated in such Plenty, as to have almost banished those with single Flowers from the Gardens.' Miller.
  GREAT BELLFLOWER, GREAT OR   *Campanula trachelium* L.
  NETTLE-LEAVED THROATWORT, CANTERBURY BELLS
Native in Europe. 'The Varieties of this are, the deep and pale blue; the white with single Flowers, and the same Colours with double Flowers . . . those with single Flowers do not merit a Place in Gardens.' Miller.
  CREEPING CAMPANULA   *Campanula rapunculoides* L.
Native in Europe and Asia Minor. Resembling *C. trachelium.* Cultivated in 1683 by James Southerland. A. R. Clapham, *et al.*, in *Flora of the British Isles*, say: 'Sometimes grown in Gardens, where it speedily becomes a weed.'

BLEW BINDWEED, CONVOLVULUS   *Ipomoea nil* (L.) Roth
Native of the Old World Tropics, but now widely distributed. There are many forms in cultivation—such as cv. 'Scarlet O'-Hara.' Miller says: 'It was cultivated before 1596 by Gerarde, but perished before it ripened its seeds . . . This species is now rarely met with in our gardens.'

BLOODROOT   *Sanguinaria canadensis* L.
Native in eastern North America. 'Cultivated in England in

1680 by Mr. William Walker . . . in St. James Street not far from St. James Palace.' Miller. Parkinson (*Theatrum botanicum*) says: 'This strange Celandine hath a fleshie roote, full of a yellow juyce, smelling strong like the ordinary, from whence rise onely three large blewish greene leaves, cut in after the manner of Vine leaves, without any foote stalke under them, or with very short ones, from among which rise a short reddish foote stalke, with a white flower on the toppe of it like unto the flower of Sowbread.'

CALENDULA *Calendula officinalis* L.
Pot Marigold. 'Native of France, in the vineyards of Italy, in the corn fields of Silesia, in orchards, gardens, and fields; flowering most part of the summer. Parkinson informs us that he received the seed of the single Marigold from Spain, where it grows wild, "by Guillaum Boel, in his time a very curious and cunning searcher of simples." It was however cultivated by Gerarde in 1597, and probably much earlier. . . . It has . . . been cultivated time out of mind in kitchen gardens for the flowers, which were dried in order to be boiled in broth: from a fancy that they are comforters of the heart and spirits. According to the observation of Linnaeus, the flowers are open from nine in the morning to three in the afternoon. This regular expansion and closing of the flowers attracted early notice, and hence this plant acquired the name of *Solsequia* and *Solis sponsa*. There is an allusion to this property in Shakespeare.

> *The Marigold, that goes to bed wi' th' sun*
> *And with him rises weeping,*

Golds or *Gouldes* is a name among the country people not only for this, but for *Chrysanthemum segatum*, any sort of Hawkweed, and in short for most yellow flowers of the syngenesia class. The varieties are supposed to have been originally obtained from the seeds of the single sort, but most of these differences continue, if the seeds are properly saved; but the two childing [bearing additional small heads around the base of the main head] Marigolds, and the largest double, are subject to degenerate, where care is not taken in saving their seeds. The best way to preserve the varieties, is to pull up all those plants, whose flowers are less double, as soon as they appear, and to save the seeds from the largest and most double flowers; the childing sort should be sown by itself in a separate part of the garden, and the seeds saved from the large center flowers only.' Miller.

Double marigold, *Calendula multiflora maxima*. From Gerarde, *Herball*.

CAMPANULA   See BELLFLOWER

CANDYTUFT, PURPLE CANDYTUFT   *Iberis umbellata* L.
Native of southern Europe. This seems to have been the commonly cultivated Candytuft of this period. It was grown by Gerarde in 1596, and was given nearly a page in Parkinson's *Paradisus*.

CANTERBURY BELLS
In the time of Parkinson (the 1600's) this referred to *Campanula trachelium* L. (see Bellflower). *C. medium* L. which we know as Canterbury Bells was at this time called Coventry Bells. 'Doubles' at this time almost surely referred to the double-flowered forms of *C. trachelium*, since double-flowered forms of *C. medium* were not common even in 1800.

CARDINAL FLOWER *Lobelia cardinalis* L.
Parkinson grew it in 1629. Dorothy S. Manks, in *Early American Nurserymen and Seedsmen*, says it 'grows naturally by the Side of Rivers and Ditches in great Part of *North America*, but has been many Years cultivated in the *European* Gardens for the great Beauty of its scarlet Flowers.'

CENTAURY *Centaurea centaurium* L.
Native in Spain and Italy. Cultivated by Gerarde in 1596. Miller says it 'stands in the List of medicinal Plants of the College, but is very rarely used; the Root is reckoned to be binding, and good for all Kinds of Fluxes, and of great use to heal Wounds.'

CENTAUREA See CENTAURY or CORNFLOWER

CELANDINE POPPY, COMMON OR *Chelidonium majus* L.
 GREAT CELANDINE
Native in Europe and northern Asia, 'flowering from may to july, during which time it is in the greatest perfection for use. . . . The juice of every part of this plant is very acrimonius It cures tetters [Herpes] and ringworms. Diluted with milk it consumes white opaque spots on the eyes. It destroys warts, and cures the itch. There is no doubt but a medicine of such activity will one day be converted to more important purposes.' Miller.

CHEQUERED LILY *Fritillaria meleagris* L.
Native in most of Europe. 'Gerarde calls it Turkey-hen or Guinea-hen flower, and Checkered Daffodill. The curious and painful herborist of Paris, John Robin, sent him many plants for his garden where they prospered (as he informs us) as in their own native country. . . .Some call it, says Parkinson, *Narcissus Caparonius* from the first finder Noel Caparon, an Apothecary then dwelling at Orleans, but shortly after murdered in the massacre of France. . . . The country people about Rislip call the flowers Snake-heads.' Miller.

CHINESE LANTERN See ALKEKENGI

CLOVE-GILLIFLOWER *Dianthus caryophyllus* L.
Native from southern Europe to India. Parkinson, in *Paradisi in sole*, says they 'grow like unto the Carnations, but not so thick set with joynts and leaves: . . ., the flowers are smaller, yet very thick and double in most.' He describes 29 varieties.

COLCHICUM, MEADOW SAFFRON *Colchicum autumnale* L.
Native in Central and Southeastern Europe. 'Mr. Miller observed it in England in great plenty, in the meadows near Castle-Bromwich in Warwickshire, the beginning of September; and says that the country people call the flowers Naked Ladies, because they come up without any leaves (They give the same name to Hepatica, and indifferently to any plant, which has flowers on naked scapes, appearing at a different time from the leaves.)' Miller. Parkinson described a double flowered variety.

COLUMBINE *Aquilegia vulgaris* L.
Temperate Europe and Asia. 'There are many sorts of Columbine as well differing in forme as colour of the flowers, and of them both single and double carefully nursed up in our Gardens, for the delight both of their forme and colours.' Parkinson, *Paradisi*.

'The root, the herb, the flowers, the seeds have been recommended to be used medicinally, on good authority; but this plant is of a suspicious tribe, and Linnaeus affirms as of his own knowledge, that children have lost their lives by an over dose of it. The virtues ascribed to a tincture of the flowers, as an anti-phlogistic, and for strengthening the gums, and deterging [cleansing] scorbutic ulcers in the mouth, appear to be better founded; the tincture being made with an addition of the vitrioloc acid [sulphuric acid], and differing little from our official tincture of roses.' Miller.

CORNFLOWER, BLEW BOTTLE, *Centaurea cyanus* L.
CORN CENTAURY
Native in most of Europe. 'It is a common weed among corn [grain], flowering from june to august, the wild flower is usually blue, but sometimes white or purple. . . . Dr. Stokes in-

forms us, that it is called Bachelor's-buttons in Yorkshire and Derbyshire: but this is a name given to many other flowers. In Scotland it is called Blue Bonnetts. . . . The expressed juice of the neutral florets makes a good ink; it also stains linen of a beautiful blue, but the colour is not permanent in any mode hitherto used. Mr. Boyle says that the juice of the central florets, with the addition of a very small quantity of alum, makes a lasting transparent blue, not inferior to ultramarine.' Miller.

CROCUS *Crocus vernus* (L.) All.
(*C. purpureus* Weston)
Native of the mountains of southern and central Europe. Parkinson listed some 29 garden varieties in *Paradisi in sole*.

CROWN IMPERIAL *Fritillaria imperialis* L.
Native from Iran to the Himalayas. 'This grows naturally in Persia, from whence it was first brought to *Constantinople*, and about the Year 1570, was introduced to these Parts of *Europe*.' 'Gerarde had great plenty of it in his garden in 1596, he calls it a rare and strange plant. Parkinson (in 1629) had not observed any variety in the colour of the flowers. Lobel, however, enumerated many varieties.' Miller. It is worth noting that by the time of Miller (1759) at least twelve garden forms had been recognized.

DAFFODILL, DAFFADOWN DILLIES, *Narcissus* sp.
    TRUMPETS, POETS, DOUBLES, MULTIPLES
    COMMON JONQUIL *Narcissus jonquilla* L.
Cultivated by Gerarde in 1596. Native in southern Europe and Algeria.
    CURTIS PRIMROSE PEERLESS *Narcissus* × *biflorus* Curtis
    NARCISSUS, PALE DAFFODIL
Probably a hybrid between *N. poeticus* and *N. tazetta*.
    POETIC, POETS, OR WHITE NARCISSUS, *Narcissus poeticus* L.
    PHEASANT'S EYE
Native of southern Europe. Cultivated in England by 1570 according to L'Obel.

POLYANTHUS NARCISSUS *Narcissus tazetta* L.
Gerarde grew it in 1596. Native from the Canary Islands to Japan. 'Clusius observed it at the end of january 1565 in Spain and Portugal and at the begining of february at Gibraltar.' Miller.

RUSH-LEAVED DAFFODIL, *Narcissus triandrus* L.
ANGELS-TEARS
'Clusius says that a French herbarist, named Nicolas le Quelt or Quilt, who searched the Pyrenees and Spain every year, introduced it in 1599.' Miller.

SWEET-SCENTED NARCISSUS, *Narcissus odorus* L.
CAMPERNELLE JONQUIL (*N. Calathinus* L.)
Native in France and Spain. 'Clusius first observed them in flower in april 1595, in the garden of Theodoric Clutius or Cluyts, prefect of the Academic Garden at Leyden.' Miller.

WILD OR COMMON DAFFODIL *Narcissus pseudonarcissus* L.
Native in western Europe from Belgium to Portugal, naturalized in Scandinavia and central Europe. Parkinson, in *Paradisi*, listed many varieties, several of them double. This is the common wild English Daffodil.

Crocus,*Crocus byzantinus; Crocus montanus.*From De Passe,*Hortus floridus.*

Great daisy, *Bellu major*. From Gerarde, *Herball*.

DAISY, GREAT DAISY, COMMON OXE-EYE   *Chrysanthemum leucanthemum* L.

Native throughout Europe. A common weed of fields. A double flowered form was known to Parkinson.

PERENNIAL OR COMMON DAISY   *Bellis perennis* L.

Native over much of Europe. 'The common Daisy, . . . grows naturally in Pasture Land in most Parts of Europe, and is often a troublesome Weed in the Grass of Gardens, so is never cultivated. . . . The Garden Daisy is generally supposed to be only a Variety of the wild Sort, which was first obtained by Culture. This may probably be true, but there has not been any Instance of late Years of the wild Sort, having been altered by Culture; for I have kept this wild Sort in the Garden upward of thirty Years, and have constantly parted the Roots, and raised many Plants from Seeds, but they have constantly remained the same; nor have I ever observed the Garden Daisy to degenerate to the wild Sort, where they have been some Years neglected, though they have altered greatly with regard to the Size and Beauty of their Flowers.' Miller.

DATURA   See THORNAPPLE

COLONIAL GARDENS

DAYLILY, YELLOW   *Hemerocallis lilio-asphodelus* L.
    ASPHODEL LILY,   emend. Hylander (*H. flava* L.)
    LIRICONFANCIE, YELLOW DAY LILY
RED ASPHODEL LILY,   *Hemerocallis fulva* L.
    ORANGE DAY LILY

Hemerocallis lilio-asphodelus L. is a native of Eastern Asia, *H. fulva* is known only in cultivation. John Gerarde, in his *Herball*, writes: 'These Lilies, ... do grow in my garden, and in the gardens of herbarists and lovers of fine and rare plants.' Parkinson and Miller both note that while *H. fulva* sets no seed, and the flowers last for but a single day, *H. lilio-asphodelus* does set seed and the individual flowers last for more than one day. Miller further notes of the seeds of *H. lilio-asphodelus* that 'if sown in Autumn, the Plants will come up the following Spring, and these will flower in two Years; but if the Seeds are not sown till Spring, the plants will not come up till the year after.' We now know that *H. fulva* is a triploid, and hence sterile, and that it is not known in a wild condition—though allied diploids are found in China.

DEAD NETTLE, RED OR PURPLE   *Lamium purpureum* L.
    DEAD NETTLE OR ARCHANGELL
WHITE ARCHANGELL   *Lamium album* L.

Native in Europe. In the time of Parkinson (1640) esteemed for medicinal uses.

DELPHINIUM See LARK'S SPUR

DIANTHUS See CLOVE-GILLIFLOWER

DIGITALIS, FOXGLOVE   *Digitalis purpurea* L.

Native in western Europe. Yields a powerful drug, poisonous in large doses. At this period used as a diuretic.

DITTANY See FRAXINELLA

DOGTOOTH VIOLET   *Erythronium dens-canis* L.

Native in central Europe. Parkinson, in *Paradisi*, writes: 'The sorts of Dens Caninus do grow in divers places; some in Italy on the *Euganean* Hills, others on the Apenine, and some about *Gratz*, the chiefe City of Stiris, and also about Bayonne, and in other places. We have had from *Virginia* a root sent unto us, that we might well judge, by the forme and colour thereof being dry, to be . . . the root of this, . . . which the naturall people hold not onely to be singular to procure lust, but hold it as a secret, loth to reveale it.'

ELECAMPANE *Inula helenium* L.
Probably native in Central Asia, but now widely naturalized in western Asia, Europe, North America and Japan. 'The root is esteemed a good pectoral, and a conserve of it is recommended in disorders of the breast and lungs, as good to promote expectoration. An infusion of it fresh, sweetened with honey, is said to be an excellent medicine in the hooping cough. A decoction of it, applied outwardly, is said to cure the itch. Bruised and macerated in urine, with balls of ashes and whortleberries [Vaccinium spp.], it dyes a blue colour.' Miller.

EMANIES See ANEMONE.

ENGLISH DAISY See DAISY

EPIMEDIUM, BARRENWORT *Epimedium alpinum* L.
Native in southern Europe. 'This rare and strange plant (says Gerarde) was sent me from the French King's herbarist, *Robinius*, dwelling in Paris, at the sign of the black head, in the street called *Du bout du Monde*. I planted it in my garden, but it was dried away with the extreme heat of the sun, which happened in the year 1590, since which time it bringeth seed to perfection.' Miller.

'The Roots if planted in a good Border, should be every Year reduced, so as to keep them within Bounds, otherwise it will spread its Roots and interfere with the neighboring Plants.' Miller.

FEVERFEW, *Chrysanthemum parthenium* (L.)
    FETHER-FEW Bernh.
Native in Europe. 'It grows naturally in Lanes, and upon the

Side of Banks, in many Parts of *England*, but is frequently cultivated in the Physic Gardens to supply the Markets, . . . the whole Plant has a strong unpleasant Odour. The Leaves and Flowers of this are used in Medicine, and are particularly appropriated to the female Sex, being of great Service in all cold flatulent Disorders of the Womb, and hysterick Affections, procuring the *Catamenia*, and expelling the Birth and Secundines.' Miller.

FOUR-O-CLOCKS   See MARVEL-OF-PERU

FOXGLOVE   See DIGITALIS

FRAXINELLA, DITTANY *Dictamnus albus* L.
Native from southern Europe to northern China. 'There are three Varieties of this Plant, one with a pale red Flower striped with purple, another with a white Flower, and one with shorter Spikes of Flowers; but as I have observed them to vary when propagated by Seeds, so I esteem them only seminal Varieties. . . . This is a very ornamental Plant for Gardens, and as it requires very little Culture, so deserves a Place in all good Gardens.' Miller.

'It is held to be profitable against the stingings of Serpentes, against contagious and pestilent diseases, and to bring down the feminine courses, for the pains of the belly, and the stone, and in Epilepticall diseases, and other cold pains of the brains: the root is the most effectual for all these, yet the seed is sometimes used.' Parkinson, *Paradisi*.

FRITILLARIA   See CHEQUERED LILLY and CROWN IMPERIAL

GERANIUM, CRANESBILL *Geranium sanguinium* L.
Native from southern Scandinavia to Portugal and Greece. 'Petals obcordate, very large, pale red, with deeper veins, hairy at the base. The whole plant frequently turns red or purple after flowering. . . . Flowering most parts of the Summer, and often introduced into gardens as an ornamental plant.' Miller.

LONG-ROOTED CRANESBILL *Geranium macrorrhizum* L.
Native from south-eastern France to Italy, Austria and the

Balkans. 'The whole plant, when rubbed, emits an agreeable odour. . . . Cultivated in the Botanic Garden at Oxford in 1658.' Miller

TUBEROUS-ROOTED CRANESBILL *Geranium tuberosum* L.
Native in southern Europe. 'The root is tuberous and round like unto the root of the *Cyclamen* or ordinary sowerbread almost, but smaller, and of a dark russet colour on the outside, and white within, which doth encrease underground, by certain strings running from the mother root into small round bulbes, like unto the roots of the earth chestnut.' Parkinson, *Paradisi*.

HERB ROBERT *Geranium robertianum* L.
Native throughout Europe and temperate Asia. Naturalized

Geranium, *Herba roberti*. From Dodoens, *A Niewe Herball*.

in the United States. 'The whole is beset with pellucid hairs. ... It has a disagreeable rank smell when bruised. ... A decoction of Herb Robert has been known to give relief in calculous cases. It is considerably astringent, and is given to cattle when they make bloody water or have the bloody flux.' Miller.

GERMANDER *Teucrium chamaedrys* L.
Native in southern and central Europe, the Near East, and Morocco. 'The Chamaedrys or Germander has been esteemed chiefly as a mild aperient and corroborant: and was recommended in uterine obstructions, intermitting fevers, rheumatism and gout. Of the last mentioned complaint the Emperor Charles the Fifth is said to have been cured, by a vinous decoction of it, with some other herbs, taken for sixty successive days.' Miller.

GLADIOLUS, CORN FLAG *Gladiolus* sp.
There are at least two 'hardy' gladioli which have been cultivated since before the time of Gerarde (1596). They are native in southern and eastern Europe. They are probably not hardy in the United States north of Virginia.
    FRENCH CORNE FLAGGE *Gladiolus communis* L.
In this the pedicels of the tubular flowers twist so that the florets form a single line of flowers one above the other.
    ITALIAN CORNE FLAGGE *Gladiolus communis* L.
This plant is similar, but the flowers flare open and are arranged in two ranks, one on each side of the rhachis.
    CORNE FLAGG OF *Gladiolus byzantinus* Miller
      CONSTANTINOPLE
The flower has larger florets than the other two; brought into cultivation by 1629.

GLOBE AMARANTH *Gomphrena globosa* L.
Native in tropical Asia. 'It was cultivated in 1714 by the Dutchess of Beaufort; but was not common in the English gardens till 1725. It was raised first in Holland about 1670. . . . The flowering heads are beautiful, and if gathered before they are too far advanced, will retain their beauty several years.' Miller.

GRAPE HYACINTH, FAIRE HAIRD   *Muscari comosus* (L.) Miller
   IACINTH (Gerarde), GREAT PURPLE FAIRE HAIRED
   IACINTH (Parkinson)
Native of western Europe and North Africa. 'The flower stalk rises about a foot (or eighteen inches) in height, round, upright, smooth, glaucous green. The lower half is naked, but the upper part has a loose raceme of flowers, frequently for a foot in length. The lower flowers are farther asunder, before they flower they are upright, but whilst they flower, and afterwards, they stand out horizontally, on pedicels half an inch in length; their colour is a yellowish green, with blue or purple at the end, these are fertile. The upper ones are smaller, barren, stand upright, form a corymb, and are blue or violet, as are also their long pedicels. . . . Gerarde, who cultivated it in 1596, calls it Faire haired Iacint; Parkinson, Great purple Faire haired Iacinth; . . . It is distinguished more by its singularity than its beauty.' Miller.

GREAT GRAPE-FLOWER   *Muscari botryoides* (L.) Miller
   (Gerarde), SKIE-COLOURED GRAPE FLOWER (Parkinson)
Native in southern Europe. 'Where it is once planted in a garden, it is not easily rooted out. . . . There are three varieties of this, one with blue, another with white, and a third with ash-coloured flowers . . . Parkinson enumerates three varieties, the white, the blush-coloured and the branched: the first is frequently imported with other bulbs from Holland; the last seems to be a curious variety and was obtained, according to Clusius, from the white.' Miller.

BLEW GRAPE FLOWER   *Muscari racemosum* (L.) Miller
Native of the south of Europe, in corn fields. 'It was cultivated by Gerarde in 1596. He calls it Blew Grape-flower; and Parkinson, darke blew Grape-flower. . . . This is much more common in our gardens than the botryoides, and flowers in april and may.' Miller.

GROUND IVY, ALE-HOOF   *Nepeta hederacea* (L.) Trev.
   (*Glechoma hederacea*)
Native from western Europe to Japan. Extensively naturalized in the eastern United States. 'It gradually expels plants which grow near it, and thus impoverishes pastures. The leaves were

formerly thrown into the vat with ale to clarify it, and to give it a flavour.' Miller. R. Dodoens, in *A Niewe Herball*, writes: 'Ground Ivie brused and put into the eares, taketh away the humming and noise of ringing sounds of the same, and is good for such as are harde of hearing.'

HELLEBORE, BLACK HELLEBORUS OR *Helleborus niger* L.
CHRISTMAS ROSE

Called "the black flower at Christmas" by William Hughes in *The Flower Garden and Compleat Vineyard* (1683). Native in central and southern Europe. 'Most, if not all the Hellebores produce very powerful effects when used medicinally.... Although many writers consider this root as a perfectly innocent and safe medicine, yet we find several examples of its poisonous effects; it should, therefore be used with proper caution. It seems to have been principally from its purgative qualities that the ancients esteemed this root such a powerful remedy in maniacal disorders.' Miller.

HEPATICA, LIVERWORT *Hepatica nobilis* Miller

Native in temperate Europe. 'These Plants are some of the greatest Beauties of the Spring; their Flowers are produced in February and March in great Plenty, before the green Leaves appear, and make a very beautiful Figure in the Borders of the Pleasure Garden, especially the double sorts.' Miller. 'The double kinde likewise hath been sent from Alphonsus Pantius out of Italy, as Clusius reporteth, and was also found in the Woods, near the Castle of Starnberg in Austria, the Lady Heusenstain's possession, as the same Clusius reporteth also.' Parkinson, *Paradisi*.

HERB ROBERT See GERANIUM

HOLLYHOCK, GARDEN OR *Althaea rosea* (L.) Cavanilles
FRENCH MALLOW

Native in China. Dodoens says: 'The great tame Mallow which beareth the beyondsea or winter rose, hath great round rough leaves.... The stalke is rounde, and groweth sixe or seven foote high or more: it beareth fayre great flowers of divers coloures, in figuere lyke to the common Mallowe or Hocke: but a great deale bigger, sometimes single, sometimes double.' 'The colours of their flowers being accidental, and the double flowers being only varieties which have risen from culture, I have not enumerated them here, but shall only mention the various colours which are commonly observed: these are white, pale, red, deep-red, blackish-red, purple, yellow and flesh colour. Besides these, I many years ago saw some plants with variegated flowers, in the garden of the late Lord Burlington in London, raised from seeds which came from China.' Miller.

HYACINTH, JACINTH, BLUE- *Endymion nonscriptus* (L.) Garcke
BELL COMMON HYACINTH, HAREBELL (*Scilla nonscripta* (L.)
Hoffmansegg and Link)
Native in western Europe. 'It adorns our woods, coppices, and hedge-rows, with its flowers in the spring months.' Miller.

GARDEN HYACINTH *Hyacinthus orientalis* L.
Native from Greece to Syria and Asia Minor. 'It is very abundant about Aleppo and Bagdat, where it flowers in February. Lepechin found it not only with purple, but with yellow flowers in Russia. With us it flowers in March and April; and was cultivated by Gerarde in 1596. Probably earlier, since neither he nor Parkinson speak of the Hyacinth as a flower then new in cultivation.' Miller. 'The roots of Hyacinthe boyled in wine and dronken, stoppeth the belly, provoketh urine, and helpeth much agaynst the venomous bitings of the field Spidder.' Dodoens.

Hyacinth, *Hyacinthus major*. From Gerarde, *Herball*.

1 *Hyacinthus comosus.*
Faire haired Iacint.

2 *Hyacinthus comosus albus.*
White haired Iacint.

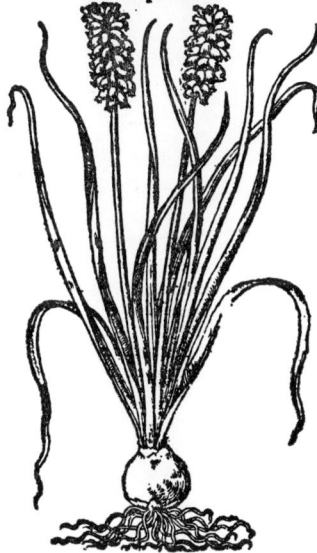

3 *Hyacinthus Botryoides cæruleus.*
Blew Grape flower.

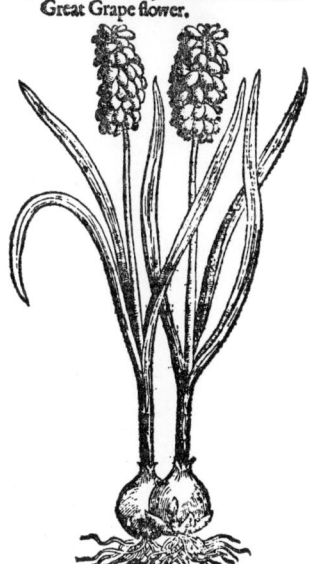

4 *Hyacinthus Botryoides cæruleus maior.*
Great Grape flower.

IRIS   *Iris* sp.
FLAG, 'BLUE AND VARIED'   *Iris pumila* L.
Native from Central Europe to Asia Minor. Cultivated by Gerarde 1596. 'There are many varieties of this sort, with white, straw-coloured, pale blue, blush-coloured, yellow-variable, blue-variable, and other colours in the flowers, which are now in great measure neglected.' Miller.

FLORENTINE IRIS,   *Iris germanica* L., var.
WHITE FLOWER DE LUCE   *florentina* (Ker.) Dykes
Cultivated by Gerarde in 1596. 'It resembles *I. germanica* very much, but differs in having the petals white and entire.' Miller.

FLOWER DE LUCE   *Iris germanica* L.
'This Flower de luce . . . is most common in gardens,' writes Parkinson in *Paradisi*.

GREAT TURKIE FLOWER DE LUCE,   *Iris susiana* L.
CHALCEDONIAN IRIS, MOURNING IRIS
Probably native in Lebanon. 'It takes the name from Susa in Persia. Clusius informs us that this magnificent Iris was brought from Constantinople to Vienna and Holland in 1573. In 1596 it was cultivated by our Gerarde.' Miller.

HUNGARIAN IRIS   *Iris sibirica* L.
The small variable Hungarian Iris of Clusius.

PERSIAN IRIS   *Iris persica* L.
Native in Asia Minor. 'Cultivated here in the time of Parkinson (1629), who remarks that it was then very rare, and seldome bore flowers. . . . Like the Hyacinth and Narcissus it will grow within doors in a water-glass, but stronger in a small pot, of sand or sandy loam, and a few flowers will scent a whole apartment.' Miller.

YELLOW FLAGG, SKEGGS, LUGS   *Iris pseudacorus* L.
Native in Europe, North Africa and Syria. 'The root of this water Flagge is very astringent, cooling and drying thereby helping all Laskes and Fluxes, whether of Blood or Humors.' Parkinson, *Theatrum botanicum*.

YELLOW FLOWER DE LUCE   *Iris variegata* L.
Cultivated by Gerarde in 1596. Considered to be one of the parents of the *I. germanica* group. 'This yellow variable Flower de luce loseth his leaves in winter, contrary to all the former Flower de luces.' Parkinson, *Paradisi*.

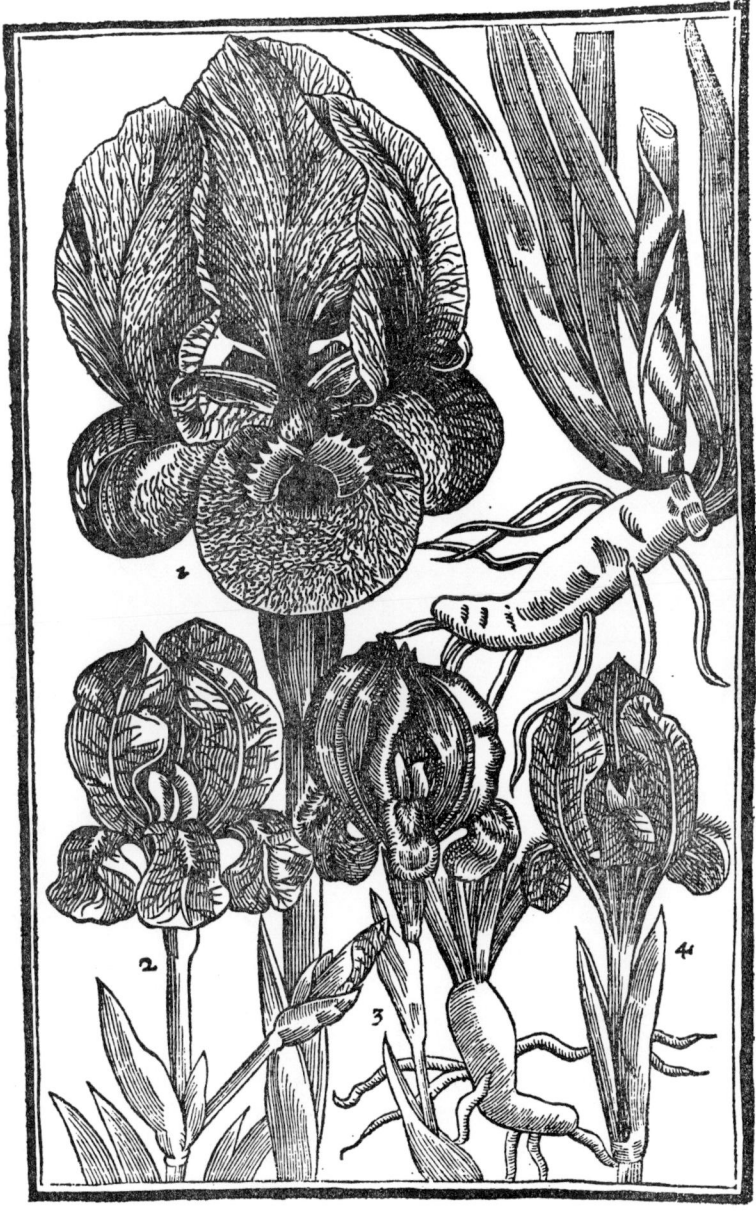

Iris, *Iris*. From Parkinson, *Paradisi in sole*.

Lark's spur, Lark's heel   *Delphinium consolida* L.
Delphinium, Lark's Claw, Lark's Toes,
Wild or Corn Lark's Spur.
Native in Europe and western Asia. 'The expressed juice of the petals, with the addition of a little alum, makes a good blue ink.' Miller.

Upright or Golden Lark's Spur   *Delphinium ajacis* L.
Native in Mediterranean region. Dodoens says: 'The seed of the garden Larckes Spurre drunken is very good agaynst the stinging of Scorpions, and in deede his vertue is so great against their poyson, that the only herbe throwen before the Scorpions, doth cause them to be without force or power to do hurte, so that they may not move or sturre, until this herbe be taken from them.'

Leucojum, Autumnal Snow-drop   *Leucojum autumnale* L.
Native in the Mediterranean region.
Summer Snow-drop, Great Late-   *Leucojum aestivum* L.
   flowering Bulbous Violet.
Native in Central and Southern Europe.

Lily   *Lilium* sp.
Common White Lily   *Lilium candidum* L.
Native from southern Europe to Southwest Asia. 'The water of the flowers distilled . . . is used . . . of divers women outwardly, for their faces, to cleanse the skin, and make it white and fresh.' Parkinson, *Paradisi*.

Martagon Imperiale   *Lilium martagon* L.
Native from southern Europe to Japan. Cultivated in 1596 by Gerarde as Martagon Imperiale.

Spotted Martagon of Canada   *Lilium canadense* L.
Native from Quebec to Virginia. 'This, says Parkinson, was brought into France from Canada by the French colony [sic], and thence unto us, in 1629. . . . It is found in other parts of North America; for Catesby says it was sent to Mr. Collinson from Pennsylvania and flowered several years in his garden.' Miller.

Lily, *Lilium*. From Fuchs, *De Historia stirpium*.

COLONIAL GARDENS 63

LILY-OF-THE-VALLEY   *Convallaria majalis* L.
Native through Europe and Asia. 'Camerarius setteth downe the manner of making an oyle of the flowers hereof, which he saith is very effectual to ease the paine of the Gout, and such like diseases, to be used outwardly, which is this; Having filled a glasse with the flowers and being well stopped, set it for a moneths space in an Ants hill, and after being drayned clear, set it by to use.' Parkinson, *Paradisi*.

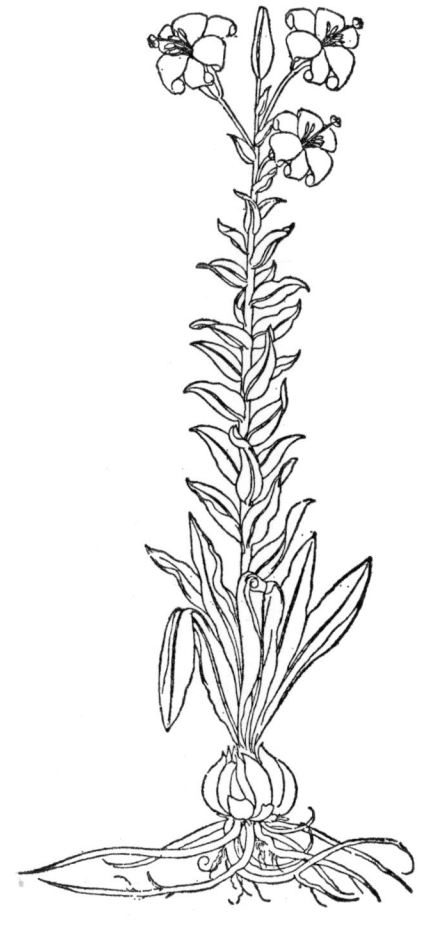

LINARIA   See TOAD-FLAX

LUNGWORT, COWSLIPS OF   *Pulmonaria officinalis* L.
   JERUSALEM
Native from Central and Northern Europe to the Caucasus. 'It is much commended of some, to be singular good for ulcered lungs, that are full of rotten matter.' Parkinson, *Paradisi*.

LUPINE   *Lupinus perennis* L.
Native from Maine to Florida. 'It is native of Virginia and other parts of North America; and was cultivated in the botanic garden at Oxford in 1658.' Miller.
   GREAT BLUE LUPINE   *Lupinus hirsutus* L.
Cultivated by Parkinson in 1629. Native in southern Europe. 'The pods are large, almost an inch broad, and three inches long.' Miller.
   WHITE LUPINE   *Lupinus albus* L.
Native in the Levant. 'Doth scoure and cleanse the skin from spots, morphew, blew marks, and other discolourings thereof, being used either in a decoction or ponther.' Parkinson, *Paradisi*.

MALLOW, FRENCH   See HOLLYHOCK

MARIGOLD, MARYGOLD,   *Tagetes patula* L.
   FRENCH MARYGOLD, *Flos Africanus, Flos Africanus Multiplex*
Native in Mexico. 'Dodoneus ... affirms that it grows spontaneously in Africa, and was first brought into Europe by the Emperor Charles V after his expedition against Tunis. But that was in the year 1535; and Fuchsius in 1542, figures the plant under the name of Tagetes indica: it has never been found in Africa. Hernandez mentions it in his history of Mexico; and the variety figured by Dillenius, which flowered in the Eltham garden in 1727, was produced from Mexican seeds ... it was common with us in Gerarde's time ... 1597.' Miller.

   AZTEC MARIGOLD, AFRICAN MARIGOLD   *Tagetes erecta* L.
Native in Mexico. Cultivated by Gerarde in 1596. 'Parkinson remarks that the flower is of the very smell of new wax, or of an

honie combe, and not of that poisonfull sent of the smaller kindes.' Miller.

MARVEL-OF-PERU   *Marabilis jalapa* L.
Native in tropical America. 'These . . . are very ornamental plants in the flower garden during the months of july, august, and september, . . . the flowers do not open till towards the evening whilst the weather continues warm, but in the moderate cool weather, when the sun is obscured, they continue open almost the whole day. . . . It was cultvated here by Gerarde many years, as he says, before the publication of his Herbal in 1597.' Miller.

MEADOW RUE, FEATHERED COLUMBINE,   *Thalictrum flavum* L.
    COMMON MEADOW RUE
Native in Europe and temperate Asia. 'A cataplasm made of the bruised leaves is a slight blister, and has been known to give relief in the Sciatica. The root dyes wool yellow.' Miller. The name 'Feathered Columbine' is used now for the *Thalictrum aquilegifolium* L., another European species. However, it seems that this did not come into cultivation in England, at least, before 1731.

MONARDA, BLUE   *Monarda fistulosa* L.
    PURPLE MONARDA, WILD BERGAMOT
Native from Quebec and Ontario to Florida and Texas. 'Cultivated in 1656 by Mr. John Tradescant, jun.' Miller.

MORNING GLORY   See BLEW BINDWEED

MULLEIN, VERBASCUM,   *Verbascum thapsus* L.
    GREAT MULLEIN OR AARON'S ROD
Native in most of Europe and western Asia, widely naturalized on dry soils, gravel banks, or pastures and the like in eastern North America. It was a common plant in fields around Boston by 1824. 'The leaves and whole herb are mucilaginous, and recommended as emollients both internally and externally. A pint of Cow's Milk with a handful of leaves, boiled in it to half a pint, sweetened with sugar, strained and taken at bed-time,

is a pleasant emollient and nutritious medicine for allaying a cough, and more particularly for taking off the pain and irritation of the piles.' Miller.

MOTH MULLEIN *Verbascum blattaria* L.
Native in temperate Europe eastward to western and central Asia, also in North Africa.

NASTURTIUM, INDIAN CRESS, *Tropaeolum majus* L.
    GREAT INDIAN CRESS
'The flowers are frequently eaten in salads; they have a warm taste like the garden cress, and hence the plant has its common name of Nasturtium; they are likewise used for garnishing dishes. The seeds are pickled, and by some are preferred to most pickles for sauces under the false name of capers.' Miller.

NIGELLA, FENNEL FLOWER *Nigella damascena* L.
Native in southern Europe. 'It was cultivated here in 1570, as appears from Lobel.' Miller.

NONESUCH   See ROSE CAMPION

PANSY, HEART'S EASE *Viola tricolor* L.
Native in northern and central Europe. 'Linnaeus remarks the black line which sometimes appears on the petals; and gave occasion to Milton's expression of "Pansies streackt with jet". . . It has ever been a favorite flower with the people.' Miller.

PELLETORY, PARITARY *Parietaria officinalis* L.
Native in eastern and central Europe. Parkinson writes, in *Theatrum*: 'The dried herbe Paritary made up with honey into an electuarie, or the juice of the herb, or the decoction thereof made up with Sugar or Hony, is a singular remedy for any old continuall or dry cough.'

PEONY, MALE PEONY, *Paeonia mascual*
    FEMALE PEONY *P. officinalis* L.   (L.) Miller
Native in southern Europe. 'There are two principall kinds of Peonie, that is to say, the Male and the Female. Of the Male

kind I have only known one sort, but of the Female a great many; . . . The Male his leaf is whole, without any particular division, notch or dent on the edge, . . . The Female of all sorts hath the leaves divided or cut on the edges.' Parkinson, *Paradisi*.

Poppy, *Papaver satiuum album*. From Gerarde, *Herball*.

POPPY, FRENCH POPPY, FIELD POPPY *Papaver rhoeas* L.
Native in Europe, Asia, and North Africa, occasionally found as an escape in eastern North America. 'There are several Varieties of this with double Flowers cultivated in Gardens; some of them have white Flowers, others have red Flowers bordered with white, and some have variegated Flowers.' Miller. The red double-flowered form was cultivated by Parkinson in 1629.

WHITE POPPY, BLACK POPPY, *Papaver somniferum* L.
OPIUM POPPY
Native in Greece and sub-tropical Asia, occasionally escaped from cultivation in eastern North America. 'It is not unknown, I suppose to any, that Poppie procureth sleepe, for which cause it is wholly and only used, as I think.' Parkinson, *Paradisi*.

PRIMROSE, COWSLIP, BEAR'S EARS   *Primula vulgaris* Hudson
Native in Europe, Asia Minor, and North Africa. Flowering peduncle lacking or very short. 'I . . . call those only Primroses that carry but one flower on a stalk, be they single or double.' Parkinson, *Paradisi*.

BEAR'S EARS   *Primula auricula* L.
Native in the Alps. 'From Gerarde's herbal it appears that the Auricula was cultivated in 1597 . . . to enumerate all the diversities of this plant would be almost endless; for every year produces vast quantities of new flowers.' Miller.

COWSLIP, PAIGLE   *Primula veris* L.
Native in Europe and temperate Asia. 'The fragrant flowers make a pleasant wine, approaching in flavour to the Muscadel wine of the South of France.' Miller.

Rose, *Rosa*. From Fuchs, *De Historia stirpium*.

RANUNCULUS   *Ranunculus asiaticus* L.
  CROWFOOT
Native in southwestern Europe and southwestern Asia. 'It was originally brought from Persia; but since it has been in Europe, many new varieties have been obtained from seeds.' Miller. It was cultivated by Gerarde in 1696; Parkinson listed eight varieties in 1629.

  GRASSY CROWFOOT   *Ranunculus gramineus* L.
'Parkinson figures it with double flowers, but describes it with semi-double ones only . . . that with single flowers was cultivated by Gerarde in 1596.' Miller.

  FAIR MAID OF FRANCE,   *Ranunculus aconitifolius* L.
    ACONITE-LEAVED CROWFOOT
Native in Central Europe, from Spain to Jugoslavia. 'The double-flowering variety has been obtained by seeds, and is preserved in many curious gardens for the beauty of its flowers. It is by some gardeners called Fair Maid of France . . . Gerarde in 1597 said "it groweth in the gardens of Herbarists, and lovers of strange plants, whereof we have good plentie." ' Miller.

  BULBOUS CROWFOOT   *Ranunculus bulbosus* L.
Native in Europe and Western Asia, naturalized throughout much of North America. 'The flowers are sometimes double . . . Like most Crowfoots it possesses the property of inflaming and blistering the skin; . . . According to Hoffmann, beggars make use of them to blister their skins with a view to exciting compassion.' Miller.

  YELLOW BATCHELOR'S BUTTONS   *Ranunculus acris* L.
The garden form is of apparently obscure origin. 'It is frequent in gardens with a double flower, among other herbaceous perennials, under the name of yellow Batchelor's Buttons.' Miller.

ROCKET, DAMES VIOLET   *Hesperis matrionalis* L.
Native in Europe and in Western and Central Asia. 'The Garden Rocket with purple flowers was formerly in greater plenty in English gardens than at present, having been long neglected because the flowers were single, and made but little

appearance: however, as they have a very grateful scent, the plant is worthy of a place in every good garden ... Gerarde in 1597 speaks of it as being then sown in gardens for the beauty of the flowers. And Johnson adds (1633) that by the industry of some of our florists, within two or three years hath been brought unto our knowledge a very beautiful kind of these Dames Violets, having very fair double white flowers.' Miller.

ROSE CAMPION, MALTESE CROSS,   *Lychnis chalcedonica* L.
    NONESUCH, FLOWER OF CONSTANTINOPLE,
    FLOWER OF BRISTOW, FLOWER OF BRISTOL
Native in Russia. 'Cultivated in 1596 by Gerarde. In his time it was common in almost every garden; but he does not mention any of the varieties. Parkinson in 1629 and Johnson in 1633 have the varieties; but the latter says that "the white and blush single and the double one are not to be found but in the gardens of our prime Florists." ' Miller.

SCABIOSA, SWEET SCABIOUS   *Scabiosa atropurpurea* L.
Native in Southern Europe. Parkinson says, in *Paradisi*: 'The sorts of Scabious being many, yeeld not flowers of beauty or respect, fit to be cherished in our garden of delight; and therefore I leave them to the Fields and Woods, there to abide. I have only two or three strangers to bring to your acquaintance, which are worthy this place.'

SEA HOLLY   *Eryngium maritimum* L.
Native on the coasts of Europe from the Baltic to the Black Sea. 'By old English writers it is called Sea Holly, Sea Holme, and Sea Hilver.' Miller.

SENSITIVE PLANT   *Mimosa pudica* L.
Native in tropical America. 'Parkinson calls it Mimick, Mocking or Thorny Sensitive Plant or shrub, and says that he saw a living plant of it in a pot at Chelsey in Sir John Davers garden, where divers seeds being sown about the middle of May 1638 and 1639, some of them sprang up to be near half a foot high.' Miller.

SNAPDRAGONS *Antirrhinum majus* L.
Native in the Mediterranean region. 'There is some diversity in the Snapdragons, some being of a larger, and others of a lesser stature and bigness; and of the larger, some of one, and some of another colour.' Parkinson, *Paradisi.*

Snapdragon, *Antirrhinum purpureum.* From Gerarde, *Herball.*

STAR OF BETHLEHEM, *Ornithogalum umbellatum*, L.
ORNITHOGALLUM
Native in the Mediterranean region. Naturalized in eastern North America from Newfoundland to Nebraska southward to North Carolina and Mississippi. 'The ordinary Star of Bethlehem is so common, and well known in all countries and places, that it is almost needless to describe it.' Parkinson, *Paradisi.*

STOCK-GILLIFLOWER,   *Matthiola incana* (L.) Robert Brown
    WALLFLOWER
Native in southern Europe, Asia Minor, and North Africa. 'The Stock-Gilliflower is of very long standing in the English Gardens. Johnson [1633] gives a figure of the double stock, which was not in Gerarde's original work, and observes that many and pretty varieties of it were kept in the garden of his kind friend Master Ralph Tuggye at Westminster: we may conclude, therefore, that double Stocks [Brompton Stocks] were not known in Gerarde's time (1596).' Miller.

STRAWFLOWERS, EVERLASTINGS   *Helichrysum stoechas* (L.) DeCandolle
Native in southern Europe. 'The whole Plant is very woolly, the Flowers terminate the Stalks, in a compound Corymbus; . . . If these are gathered before the Flowers are much opened, the Heads will continue in Beauty many years, especially if they are kept from the Air and Dust.' Miller.

    AMERICAN EVERLASTING,   *Anaphalis margaritacea* (L.)
       CUDWEED   Bentham
Native in North America. 'A decoction of the flowers and stalks is used in America, to foment the limbs, for pains and bruises.' Miller.

SUNFLOWER   *Helianthus annuus* L.
Native in Western North America. 'Sometimes the heads of the Sun-flower are dressed, and eaten as Hartichokes are, and are accounted of some to be good meat, but they are too strong for my taste.' Parkinson, *Paradisi*.

SWEET JOHN   See ARMERIA

SWEET PEAS, PERENNIAL   *Lathyrus latifolius* L.
Native in southern Europe. 'It is a showy plant for shrubberies, wilderness quarters, arbours, and trellis work; but too large and rampant for the borders of the common flower garden.' Miller.

SWEET WILLIAM   See ARMERIA

THORNAPPLE, JIMSON WEED   *Datura stramonium* L.
Native in tropical Asia, widely naturalized in North America. 'That it is a native of America . . . we have the most undoubted proofs, . . . Kalm says that it grows about the villages and that this and the Phytolacca are the worst there.' Miller.

TOAD FLAX, WILD FLAX   *Linaria vulgaris* Miller
Europe and western Asia, naturalized in the United States. 'In Worcestershire it is called Butter and Eggs. Gerarde names it Wild Flaxe, Tode Flaxe, and Flaxweede. . . . The juice, mixed with milk, is a poison to flies.' Miller.

TOMATO   *Lycopersicum esculentum* Miller
Native in Peru and Ecuador. 'In the hot countries where they naturally grow, they are much eaten of the people, to cool and quench the heat and thirst of their hot stomachs . . . we only have them for curiosity in our gardens, and for the amorous aspect or beauty of the fruit.' Parkinson, *Paradisi*.

TULIPS   *Tulipa gesneriana* L.
'DOUBLES AND SINGLES'   *Tulipa clusiana* DeCandolle
Native in Asia Minor. 'Conrad Gesner first made the eastern Tulip known by a description and figures . . . he tells us that he first saw it in the beginning of april 1559 at Augsbourg, in the garden of John Henry Harwart. . . . Balbinus asserts that Busbequius brought the first Tulip roots to Prague, whence they were spread all over Germany . . . the Tulip was cultivated in England by Mr. James Garret, in 1577.' Miller. 'Broken' types were commonly requested. These, it will be recalled, are the result of a virus infection.

VALERIAN, OFFICIAL OR   *Valeriana officinalis* L.
    GREAT WILD VALERIAN
Native in temperate Europe and Asia. 'It is well known that cats are much delighted with the roots. Dr. Stokes informs us that rats are equally fond of them, and that rat-catchers employ them to draw the rats together.' Miller.
    RED VALERIAN   *Kentranthus ruber* (L.) DeCandolle
Native in Central and Southern Europe, North Africa and

Asia Minor. 'Gerarde says it grew plentifully in his garden, being a great ornament to the same, and not common in England. Parkinson, that it grows in our gardens chiefly, for we know not the natural place of it.' Miller.

VIOLETS, SWEET VIOLETS *Viola odorata* L.
Native in most of Europe, Asia Minor and North Africa. 'The Garden Violets (for the wild I leave to their owne place) are so well known unto all, that either keep a garden, or have but once come into it, that I shall (I think) but lose labour and time to describe that which is so common.' Parkinson, *Paradisi*. 'The flowers of violets, taken in the quantity of a dram or two, act as a mild laxative. . . . The syrup is very useful in chemistry, to detect an acid or an alkali; the former changing the blue colour to a red, and the latter to a green.' Miller.

WALLFLOWERS, KEIRI *Cheiranthus cheiri* L.
Probably native in the Eastern Mediterranean region. 'The common Wall-flower . . . is common on old walls and buildings in many parts of England. It is one of the few flowers which have been cultivated for their fragrancy time immemorial, in our gardens.' Miller.

YARROW *Achillea millefolium* L.
Native in Europe and Western Asia. Naturalized in North America. Common in fields and pastures around Boston by 1824. 'The inhabitants of Dalekarlia mix it with their ale, instead of hops, in order to increase the inebriating quality of the liquor . . . an ointment is made of it for the piles and it is reckoned good against the scab in sheep.' Miller.

YUCCA *Yucca gloriosa* L.
Native along the coast from North Carolina to Florida. 'First cultivated in Europe by John Gerarde, who had it from the West Indies, "by a servant of a learned and skilful Apothecare of Excester, named Master Thomas Edwards". Parkinson adds, that Gerarde kept it to his death, but that it perished with him who got it from his widow, intending to send it to his country

house. Gerarde sent it to Robin at Paris, and Vespasian the son of old Robin sent it to Master John de Franqueville, which plant was flourishing in Parkinson's Garden when he published his Paradisus in 1629.' Miller.

Violet, *Violae nigrae*. From Brunfels, *Herbarum vivae eicone*.

II Herbs, Aromatic, Culinary and Medicinal, before 1700

ALKANET, BUGLOSS   *Anchusa sempervirens* L.
Native in southern Europe. Cultivated in Britain for many years.

ANGELICA   *Angelica archangelica* L.
Native in Europe and Asia. Cultivated in Britain in 1568.

ANISE   *Pimpinella anisum* L.
Native from Greece to Egypt. Cultivated in Britain in 1551.

BALM, BAUM   *Melissa officinalis* L.
Native in the Mediterranean region. Cultivated in Britain by 1596.

BASIL   *Ocimum basilicum* L.
Native in the Old World tropics. Cultivated in Britain in 1596.

BEE-FLOWER   *Ophrys apifera* Hudson
Native in Britain. Collected, but probably not cultivated, as a source of Salep.

BORAGE   *Borago officinalis* L.
Native in Europe and North Africa. Long cultivated in Britain.

BURNETT   *Sanguisorba officinalis* L.
Native in Europe and Asia. Both long used in Britain.

COLONIAL GARDENS 77

CARAWAY *Carum carvi* L.
Native in Europe. Long cultivated.

CASTMARY, BIBLELEAF *Chrysanthemum balsamita* L.
Native in western Asia. Long cultivated.

CATNIP, CATMINT *Nepeta cataria* L.
Native in Europe and west and central Asia. Long cultivated.

Basil, *Basilicum*. From Brunfels, *Herbarum vivae eicone*.

CHAMOMILE *Anthemis nobilis* L.
Native in Europe, North Africa and the Azores. Long cultivated.

CHERVIL *Anthriscus cerefolium* (L.) Hoffman
Native in eastern Europe, and southern and central Asia. Cultivated in Britain in 1597.

CHIVES, CIVES, CHIBBALS *Allium schoenoprasium* L.
Native in Europe and Asia. Cultivated in Britain in 1597.

CLARY *Salvia sclarea* L.
Native in southern Europe. Cultivated in Britain in 1562.

COMFREY *Symphytum officinale* L.
Native in Europe and Asia. Long cultivated.

CORIANDER *Coriandrum sativum* L.
Probably native in the eastern Mediterranean region. Long cultivated.

CRESS *Lepidium sativum* L.
Native in western Asia. Long cultivated.

DILL *Anethum graveolens* L.
Native in Europe. Cultivated in Britain in 1597.

DOCK, PATIENCE DOCK, RHUBARB *Rumex patientia* L.
Native in Europe, western Asia and North Africa. Cultivated in Britain in 1597.

FENNEL *Foeniculum vulgare* Miller
Native in the Mediterranean region. Long cultivated.

FLAX *Linum usitatissimum* L.
Origin unknown. Long cultivated.

HOUSELEEK Probably *Sempervivum tectorum* L.
Origin unknown. Naturalized all over Europe. Long cultivated.

Hyssop, Isop *Hyssopus officinalis* L.
Native in southern Europe and western Asia. Cultivated in Britain in 1596.

Coriander, *Coriandrum*. From Brunfels, *Herbarum vivae eicone*.

Lavender *Lavandula officinalis* Chaix
Native in the Mediterranean region. Cultivated in Britain in 1568.

Licorice, Liquorice *Glycyrrhiza glabra* L.
Native in the Mediterranean region. Cultivated in Britain in 1558.

Lovage *Levisticum officinale* K. Koch
Native in southern Europe. Cultivated in Britain in 1596.

Madder *Rubia tinctorum* L.
Native in the Mediterranean region. Cultivated in Britain in 1597.

Marjoram, Sweet *Majorana hortensis* Moench
Native in Europe. Long cultivated.

MINTS, GARDEN MINTS
Native in Europe. Long cultivated.
 CORN MINT   *Mentha arvensis* L.
 HORSE MINT   *Mentha longifolia* Hudson
                (*M. sylvestris* L.)
 PENNYROYAL   *Mentha pulegium* L.
 PEPPERMINT   *Mentha piperata* L.
 SPEARMINT   *Mentha spicata* L. (*M. viridis* L.)

MUSTARD   *Brassica nigra* (L.) K. Koch
Naturalized throughout south and central Europe. Long cultivated.

PARSLEY   *Petroselinum crispum* (Miller) Nymann
           var. *latifolium* (Miller) Airy-Shaw
Native in southern Europe. Long cultivated.

PURSLANE   *Portulaca oleracea* L.
Cosmopolitan weed of warm climate. Cultivated in Britain, 1562.

RHUBARB   *Rheum rhaponticum* L.
Native in Siberia. Cultivated in Britain in 1629.

ROSEMARY   *Rosmarinus officinalis* L.
Native in southern Europe. Long cultivated.

RUE   *Ruta graveolens* L.
Native in southern Europe. Long cultivated.

SAFFRON   *crocus sativus* L.
Probably native in Asia Minor. Long cultivated.

SAGE   *Salvia officinalis* L.
Native in the Mediterranean region. Cultivated in Britain in 1597.

SANTOLINA, LAVENDER COTTON   *Santolina chamaecyparissus* L.
Native in the Mediterranean region. Cultivated in Britain in 1596.

Savory, Summer   *Satureja hortensis* L.
   Savory, Winter   *S. montana* L.
Native in Europe. Cultivated in Britain in 1562.

Skirret   *Sium sisarum* L.
Native in eastern Asia. Cultivated in Britain in 1597.

Sorrel   *Rumex acetosa* L.
Native in the North Temperate Zone. Long used.

Southernwood   *Artemesia abrotanum* L.
Native in Europe. Cultivated in Britain in 1596.

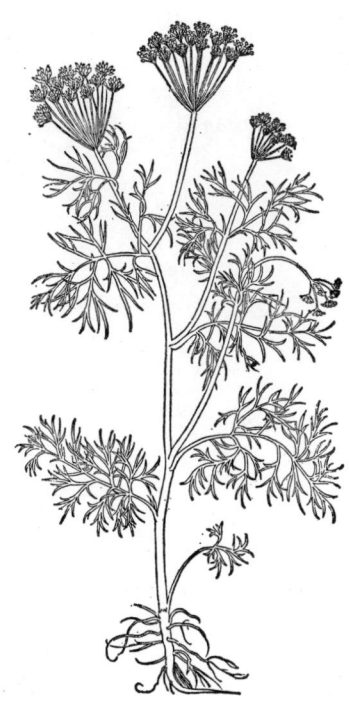

Dill, *Anethum*. From Fuchs, *De Historia stirpium*.

82　　　　　　　　*HERBS FOR*

Sweet Cicely　　　　　　　　　*Myrrhis odorata* (L.)
　　　　　　　　　　　　　　　　　　Scopoli
Native in Europe. Cultivated in Britain in 1597.

Tansy　　　　　　　　　　　　*Tanacetum vulgare* L.
Native in Europe and Asia. Long cultivated.

Summer savory, *Satureja hortensis aftiva*. From Gerarde, *Herball*.

Tarragon　　　　　　　　　　*Artemesia dracunculus* L.
Native in Europe. Cultivated in Britain in 1596.

Thyme, Time　　　　　　　　　*Thymus serpyllum* L.
Native in northern Europe. Long cultivated.

GARDEN THYME   *Thymus vulgaris* L.
Native in southern Europe. Cultivated in Britain in 1596.

TOBACCO   *Nicotiana tabacum* L.
                                         N. rustica L.
Native in tropical America. Introduced to Britain by 1570.

WOAD   *Isatis tinctoria* L.
Native in central and southern Europe. Cultivated since prehistoric time.

YARROW   *Achillea millefolium* L.
Native in Europe and western Asia. Long cultivated.

III Vegetables and Field Crops before 1700

ARTICHOKE   *Cynara scolymus* L.
Miller says, in his *Gardener's Dictionary:* 'In some parts it is eaten raw in its wild state, by the common people, and surely, must be a most wretched food. It is said to dye a good yellow: and the flowers are used instead of rennet to turn milk for cheese. . . . We learn from Turner that the Artichoke was certainly cultivated in England in 1551. We probably had it sooner.'

ARTICHOKE, JERUSALEM   *Helianthus tuberosus* L.
Cultivated in England at least by 1617. Parkinson writes, in *Paradisi in sole:* 'We in England, from some ignorant and idle head, have called them Artichokes of Jerusalem, only because the root, being boiled, is in taste like the bottom of an artichoke head; the Franks brought them first from Canada into these parts . . . [they] . . . are by reason of their great increasing, grown to be so common here with us at London, that even the most vulgar begin to despise them, where as when they were first received among us, they were dainties for a queen.'

ASPARAGUS, SPERAGE   *Asparagus officinalis* L.
'The first shoots or heads of Asparagus are a Sallet of much esteem with all sorts of persons, as any other whatsoever, being boiled tender, and eaten with butter, vinegar, and pepper, oyl and vinegar, or as every ones manner doth please; and are almost wholly spent for the pleasure of the palate. It is specially good to provoke urine, and for those that are troubled with

stone or gravel in the veins or kidneys, because it doth a little open and cleanse those end parts.' Parkinson, *Paradisi*.

BARLEY *Hordeum vulgare* L.
'The ancients fed their horses with barley, as we do with oats. It was eaten also in bread by the lower sort of people; and the Gladiators were called *Hordearei*, from their feeding on this grain.' Miller.

BEANS, FRENCH OR KIDNEY BEANS *Phaseolus vulgaris* L.
Cultivated in England in the time of Gerarde, 1596. 'The Garden Beans serve (as I said before) more for the use of the poor than of the rich. I shall therefore only shew you the order the poor take with them, . . . They are only boyled in fair water and a little salt, and afterwards stewed with some butter, a little vinegar and pepper being put into them, and so eaten. . . . The Kidney Beans boyled in water, husk and all, onely the ends cut off, and the string taken away, and stewed with butter, are esteemed more savory meat to many mens palates, than the former, and are a dish more often times at rich mens Tables than at the poor.' Parkinson, *Paradisi*.

BEANS, SCARLET *Phaseolus coccineus* L.
Cultivated in 1633 by John Tradescent. 'The Scarlet Beane riseth up with sundry branches twining about stakes that are set for it to runne thereon, still turning contrary to the Sunne, having three leaves on a foote stalke, . . . the flowers are for fashion like unto the rest, but are many more set together, and of a most orient scarlet color: the Beanes are larger than the ordinary kinde, and of a deepe purple turning to be blacke when is ripe and drie.' Parkinson, *Theatrum botanicum*.

BEETS *Beta vulgaris* L.
'The roots of the Roman red Beet being boyled, are eaten of divers while they are hot with a little oyle and vinegar, and is accounted a delicate sallet for the winter; and being cold they are so used and eaten likewise.' Parkinson, *Paradisi*.

BUCKWHEAT *Fagopyrum esculentum* Moench
It is now generally sowen in most of these Northerne Coun-

tries, where for the use and profit is made of it many fields are sowen there with, . . . and will not refuse to grow in an hungry ground, but is held generally to bee as good as a dunging to the ground where on it is sowen, the straw thereof also being turned in thereto.' Parkinson, *Theatrum*.

CABBAGE *Brassica oleracea* L. var. *capitata* L.

'They are most usually boyled in poudered beef broth until they be tender, and then eaten with much fat put among them . . . In the cold Countries of Russia and Muscovia, they pouder up a number of Cabbages, which serve them, especially the poorer sort, for their most Ordinary food in winter; and although they stink most grievously, yet to them they are ac-

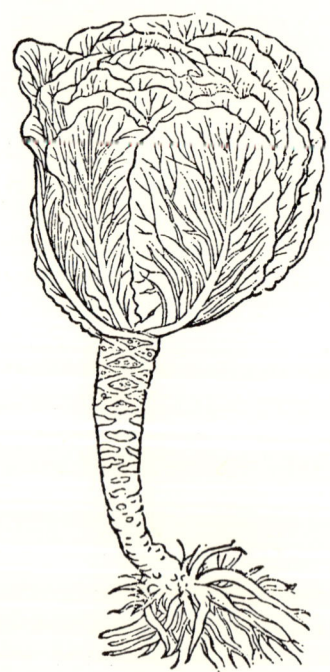

Cabbage, *Brassica tritiana*. From Dodoens, *A Niewe Herball*.

counted good meat.' 'The *Savoy* Cabbage, one is of a deeper green coloured-leaf, and curled when it is to be gathered.' Parkinson, *Paradisi*.

CARROT *Daucus carota* L.
'The carrot hath many winged leaves ... of a deep green colour, some where of in autumn will turn to be of a fine red or purple (the beauty whereof allureth many Gentlewomen oftentimes to gather the leaves, and stick them in their hats or heads, or pin them on their arms instead of feathers).' Parkinson, *Paradisi*.

CAULIFLOWER, COLE-FLOWER *Brassica oleracea* L. var. *botrytis* L.
'The Cole-flower is a kind of Cole-wort, whose leaves are large, and like the cabbage leaves, but somewhat smaller, and indented about the edges, in the middle whereof, sometimes in the beginning of Autumn, and sometimes much sooner, there appeareth a hard head of whitish yellow tufts of flowers, closely thrust together, but never open, nor spreading much with us, which then is fittest to be used, . . . this hath a much pleasanter taste than either the Cole-wort, or cabbage of any kind, and is therefore of the more regard and respect at good men's tables.' Parkinson, *Paradisi*.

CORN *Triticum* sp.
One of the most confusing common names in English is 'corn.' In Britain, and in colonial times in America, the name was a general term for field grains, most generally wheat. *Zea maize* in the time of Parkinson was Indian or Turkie Wheat, or Maize.

CUCUMBER, 'COWCUMBERS' *Cucumis sativus* L.
Cultivated in the time of Gerarde, 1566. 'Some used to cast a little salt on their sliced Cowcumbers, and let them stand half an hour or more in a dish, and then powr away the water that cometh from them by the salt, and after put vinegar, oyl, etc. thereon, as every one liketh.' Parkinson, *Paradisi*.

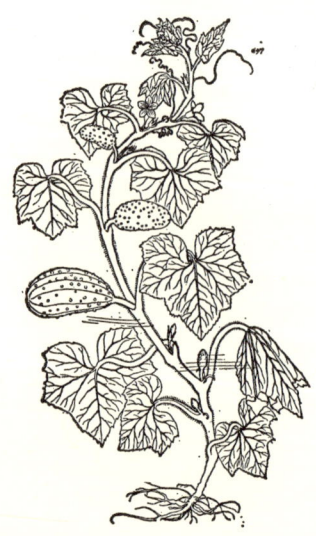

Cucumber, *Cucumber*. From Fuchs, *De Historia stirpium*.

DANDELION *Taraxacum officinale* Weber

Miller writes: 'There are four or five Species of this Genus, which grow naturally in the Fields, so are not cultivated in Gardens; but some People in the Spring gather the Roots out of the Fields, and blanch them in their Gardens for a Sallad Herb; however, as they are not cultivated, I shall forbear saying any Thing more of them, than that they are very bad Weeds both in Gardens and Fields, so should be rooted out before their Seeds are ripe.' 'Early in the spring, whilst the leaves are hardly unfolded, they are no bad ingredients in salads. The French eat the roots, and the leaves blanched, with bread and butter. Its diuretic effects have given it a vulgar name, not only in England, but other European nations.' Parkinson, in *Theatrum*, says: 'It wonderfully openeth the uritoric parts, causing abundance of urine, not only in children whose meseraical veins are not sufficiently strong to containe the quantitie of urine drawne in the night, but that then without restraint or keeping it backe they water their beds, but in those of old age also upon the stopping or yeelding small quantitie of urine.'

COLONIAL GARDENS 89

ENDIVE   *Cichorium endivia* L.
Cultivated in 1562. 'Endive being whited . . . usually being buried a while in sand, . . . is much used in winter as a sallet herb, with great delight.' Parkinson, *Paradisi*.

SUCCORY, CHICORY   *Cichorium intybus* L.
'Although Succorie be somewhat more bitter in taste than the Endives, yet it is often times, and of many eaten green, but more usually being buried a while in sand, that it may grow white, which causeth it to lose both some part of the bitterness, or also to the more tender in the eating.' Parkinson, *Paradisi*.

GARLIC   *Allium sativum* L.
'It being well boyled in salt broth, is often eaten of them that have strong stomachs, but will not brook in a weak and tender stomach.' Parkinson, *Paradisi*.

GOURDS   See also MELON,   *Cucurbita lagenaria* L.
    PUMPKIN, and SQUASH   *Lagenaria vulgaris* Ser.
'Fruit shaped like a bottle, with a large roundish belly and a neck, very smooth, when ripe of a pale yellow colour, some near six feet long, and eighteen inches round; the rind becomes hard, and being dried, contains water. . . . The Arabians call the bottle Gourd *Charrah*. The poor people eat it boiled, with vinegar; or fill the shell with rice and meat, and thus making a kind of pudding of it.' Miller.

HEMP   *Cannabis sativa* L.
'The Manured Hempe (which is of so great use, both for linnen cloath and cordage) is as I sayd of two sorts, male and female . . . to shew you the manner of steeping, drying, beating, and clensing hereof, to be made into cloth or cordage, is not my purpose or pertenent for this work; besides that, it would take up too much roome and time; it is familiarly known to every country housewife almost.' Parkinson, *Theatrum*.

HOPS   *Humulus lupulus* L.
'The young shoots are eaten early in the spring as asparagus, . . . The herb will dye wool yellow. From the stalks a strong cloth is made in Sweden.' Miller. 'The ale which our fore-

fathers were accustomed onely to drinke, being a kinde of thicker drinke than beere (caused a stranger to say of it . . . there is no drinke thicker that is drunke, there is no Urine cleerer that is made from it, it must needes be therefore that it leaveth much behind it in the belly) is now almost quite left off to be made, the use of Hoppes to be put therein, altering the quality thereof, to be much more healthfull, or rather physicall, to preserve the body from the repletion of grosse humors, which the Ale engendered.' Parkinson, *Theatrum*.

INDIAN OR TURKIE CORNE, MAIZE *Zea mays* L.
Cultivated in England in 1562. 'Is cultivated in North America and Germany. . . . The most common colour is a yellowish white; but there are some with deep yellow, others with purple, and some with blue grains; in Italy, Germany, and North America it is the food of the poor inhabitants. The Corn is ground to flour, and the poorest sort of people in America . . . make their bread of this flour; . . . this grain seldom agrees with those who have not been accustomed to eat it; however, in times of scarcity of other grain, this would be a better substitute for the poor than Bean flour.' Miller.

LEEKS *Allium porrum* L.
Cultivated by Gerarde in 1596. 'The old world, as we find in Scripture, in the time of the children of *Israel's* being in Egypt, and no doubt long before, fed much upon Leeks, Onions and Garlick boyled with flesh; and the antiquity of the Gentiles relate the same manner of feeding on them, to be in all countries the like, which howsoever our dainty age now refuseth wholly in all sorts except the poorest.' Parkinson, *Paradisi*.

LETTUCE *Lactuca sativa* L.
Mentioned by Turner in 1562.'All sorts of Lettuce are spent in Sallets, with oyl and vinegar, or as everyone please, for the most part, while they are fresh and green, or whited, as is declared in some of the sortes before, to cause them to eat the more delicate and tender. They are also boyled, to serve for many sorts of dishes of meat, as the Cooks know best.' Parkinson, *Paradisi*.

MELON CITRALL, OR   *Citrullus lanatus*
TURKIE MELON, WATERMELON   (Thunberg) Mansfield
Cultivated in 1597 by Gerarde. 'This fruit should be eaten by Europeans with great caution; when taken in the heat of the day, whilst the body is warm, colics and other bad consequences often insue; and it is well known that persons are much troubled with worms, at the time this fruit is in season.' Miller.

MUSK MELON   *Cucumis melo* L.
'They have been formerly only eaten by great personages, because the fruit was not only delicate but rare; and therefore divers were brought from *France*, and since were nursed up by the Kings or Noblemens Gardiners only, to serve for their Masters delight; but now divers others that have skill and conveniency of ground for them, do plant them and make them more common.' Parkinson, *Paradisi*.

Muskmelon, *Melo*. From Gerarde, *Herball*.

OATS *Avena sativa* L.

'The meal of this grain makes tolerable good bread, and is the common food of the country people in the north [of Britain]. In the south it is esteemed for pottage, and other messes, and in some places they make beer with it.' Miller.

ONIONS *Allium cepa* L.

'Onions are used many wayes, as sliced and put into pottage, or boyled and peeled and laid in dishes for sallets at supper, or sliced and put into water, for a sawce for Mutton or Oysters, or into meat roasted being stuffed with Parsley, and so many ways that I cannot recount them.' Parkinson, *Paradisi*.

PARSLEY *Petroselinum crispum* (Miller) Nym.

'Parsley is much used in all sorts of meats, being boyled, roasted, fryed, stewed, and being green, it serveth to lay upon sundry meats, as also to draw meat withall.' Parkinson, *Paradisi*.

PARSNIP *Pastinaca sativa* L.

'The Parsnep root is a great nourisher, and is much more used in this time of *Lent*, being boyled and stewed with butter, than in any other time of the year; yet it is very good all the winter long.' Parkinson, *Paradisi*.

PEAS *Pisum sativum* L.

'Pease of all or the most of these sorts, are either used when they are green, and be a dish of meat for the table of the rich as well as the poor, yet every one observing his time, and the kind: the fairest, sweetest, youngest, and earliest, for the better sort, the later and meaner kind for the meaner, who do not give the dearest price: or Being dry, they serve to boyl into a kind of broth or pottage, wherein many do put Tyme, Mints, Savory, or some other such hot herbs, to give it the better rellish, and is much used in Town and Country in the Lent time.' Parkinson, *Paradisi*.

POTATO *Solanum tuberosum* L.

These and the sweet potato *Ipomoea batatas* are much confused in early accounts; however, they seem to have been cultivated in Virginia in 1609. They are said to have been introduced into Ireland either in 1565 by Hawkins or 1584 by Sir Walter Raleigh. Gerarde had the potato in his garden in London in 1597. In *Sturtevant's Notes on Edible Plants*, ed. U. P. Hedrick, we are told: 'Potatoes are said to have been introduced into New England by a colony of Presbyterian Irish who settled in Londonderry, New Hampshire, in 1719, but cultivation did not become general for many years.'

PUMPKINS, POMPIONS *Cucurbita pepo* L.
Cultivated before 1570 according to L'Obel. 'They use likewise to take out the inner watery substance with the seeds, and fill up the place with Pippins [apples], and having laid on the cover which they cut off from the top, to take out the pulp, they bake them together, and the poor of the City, as well as of the Country people, do eat thereof as of a dainty dish.' Parkinson, *Paradisi*.

RADISH *Raphanus sativus* L.
'Raddishes do serve usually as a stimulum before meat, giving an appetite there unto; the poor eat them alone with bread and salt.' Parkinson, *Paradisi*.

RAMPION *Campanula rapunculus* L.
Cultivated by Gerarde in 1596. Native in Europe from the Netherlands southwards. 'The fleshy roots are eatable, and are much cultivated in France for salads. Some years past it was cultivated in English gardens for the same purpose, but is now generally neglected.... The roots are eaten not only raw in salads, but boiled like Asparagus. They were boiled tender and eaten cold with vinegar and pepper in the time of Parkinson.' Miller.

RYE *Secale cereale* L.
'Rye is of a more clammy substance than Wheate, and neither is digested so quickly, nor nourished so well, yet is accounted to be next in goodnesse unto Wheate, especially if the corne [grain] be sweet and good, and the bread well fermented and baked.' Parkinson, *Theatrum*.

94   *VEGETABLES & FIELD CROPS FOR*

SPINACH, SPINAGE   *Spinacia oleracea* L.
'Spinage is an herb fit for sallets, and for divers other purposes for the table only; for it is not known to be used physically at all.' Parkinson, *Paradisi*.

SQUASH, SUMMER SQUASH   *Cucurbita pepo* L. var.
   melopepa (L.) Alef.
'The word "squash" seems to have been derived from the American aborigines and in particular from those tribes occupying the northeastern Atlantic Coast. . . . The distinctions between the various forms of cucurbits seem to have been kept in mind by the vernacular writers, who did not use the words pompion [pumpkin] and gourd, as synonyms. . . . The word "squash" in its early use, we may conclude, applied to those varieties of cucurbits which furnish a summer vegetable and was carefully distinguished from the pumpkin. . . . At the present time, the word squash is used only in America, gourds, pumpkins, and marrows being the equivalent English names, and the American use of the word is so confusing that it can only be defined as applying to those varieties of cucurbits which are grown in gardens for table use; the word pumpkin applies to those varieties grown in fields for stock purposes; and the word gourd to those ornamental forms with a woody rind and bitter flesh, or to the Lagenaria.' Sturtevant.

SUCCORY, See ENDIVE

TURNIP   *Brassica rapa* L.
'Being boyled in salt broth, they all of them eat most kindly, and by reason of their sweetness are much esteemed, and often seen as a dish at good men's tables: but the greater quantity of them are spent at poor men's feasts.' Parkinson, *Paradisi*. Turnips are said to have been introduced into England from Holland in 1550. They were reported to be in cultivation in Massachusetts in 1629.

WHEAT   *Triticum aestivum* L.
Wheat was an unimportant grain in England as late as the

reign of the first Elizabeth. It was ordered, from England, by the Plymouth Colony in 1629. By that time it seems to have been widely grown in England in many varieties.

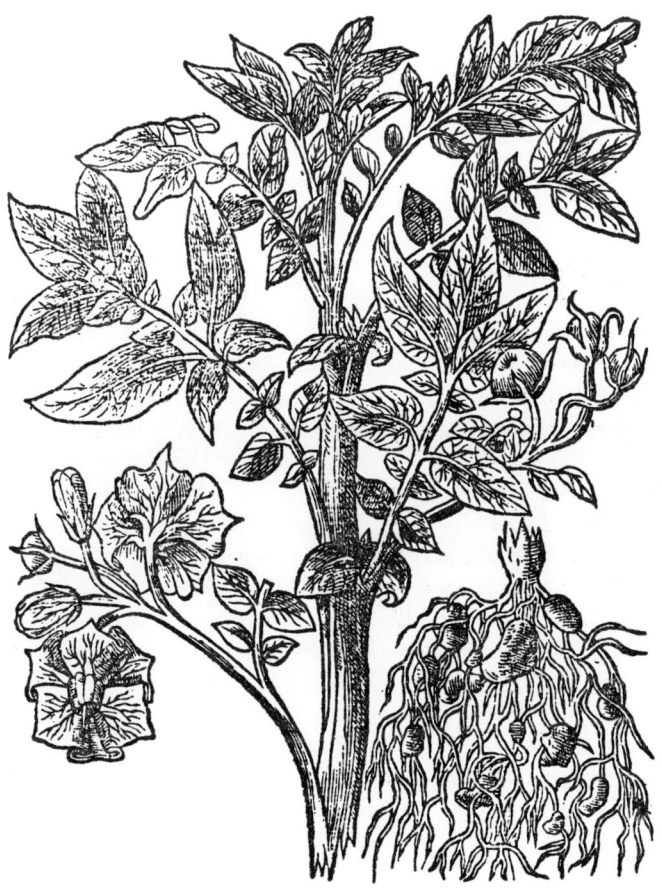

Virginia potato, *Battata virginiana*. From Gerarde, *Herball*.

IV Shrubs, Trees and Vines before 1700

ALTHEA, SHRUB MALLOW *Hibiscus syriacus* L.
Hibiscus mutabilis L.
Parkinson illustrates (but does not discuss) an *Althea frutex* which seems to be *Hibiscus syriacus*. His *Althea arborescens Provincialis* seems to be *Hibiscus mutabilis* and his *Althea frutex flore albo vel purpureo* seems to be a mixture of the two species.

ARBOR-JUDAE, JUDAS TREE, *Cercis siliquastrum* L.
SALLAD TREE possibly also *Cercis canadensis* L.
Miller, in *The Gardener's Dictionary*, says: 'The wood of the Tree is very beautifully veined with black and green, and takes a fine polish.' In 1759, he says of *C. siliquastrum*: 'The pods are gathered and used with other raw vegetables by the Greeks and Turks in salads, to which they give an agreeable odor and taste. The flowers are also made into fritters with batter and the flowerbuds are pickled in vinegar.' Of *Cercis canadensis* Sturtevant says: 'The French Canadians use the flowers in salads and pickles.'

ARBORVITAE *Thuja occidentalis* L.
'Being reckoned the most durable wood in Canada, inclosures of all kinds are scarcely made with any other wood; especially the posts which are driven into the ground. The palisades round the forts are made of this wood. . . . Clusius says that he first saw this tree in the Royal Garden at Fontainebleau, whither it was sent from Canada as a present to Francis the First.' Miller.

BAYBERRY, WAX MYRTLE *Myrica cerifera* L.
Myrica pensylvanica Loisel.
Newfoundland to North Carolina. *Myrica cerifera* is found from Delaware to Florida and *M. pensylvanica* from Newfoundland to North Carolina. 'Candles of this kind do not easily bend or melt in summer, as common candles do; they burn better and slower, nor do they cause any smoak ... A soap is made from the fat which has an agreeable scent, and is excellent for shaving.' Miller.

BLADDER-NUT *Staphylea pinnata* L.
John Parkinson, in *Theatrum botanicum*, writes: 'The Nuts are ...loathsome and overturning their stomakes that eate them, although *Scaliger* commendeth them ..., but wee will give him leave to please his palate, and stomacke with them, and will not envy the good he shall get by them, we never yet could learne that they were accepted among our people, except with some strong clownish stomache, which can almost digest an horse naile.'

BOX, ENGLISH *Buxus sempervirens* L.
'The Boxe tree ... is found with us in many woods, and wood grounds among other sorts of trees, it is also planted in divers Orchards or house backe sides, where it never groweth high, but serveth as a bush to dry Linnen on.' Parkinson, *Theatrum*.

'It was second to the Yew with us in former times for the purpose of being clipped into the shape of animals. ... The branches were in request among our ancestors for decking up houses; they are still seen among other evergreens in churches at Christmas, and in some countries they are borne by attendants at funerals.' Miller.

'The low or dwarf Box is of excellent use to border up a knot or the long beds in a Garden, being a marvelous fine ornament thereunto, in regard it groweth low, is ever green, and by cutting may be kept in what manner everyone please.' Parkinson, *Paradisi in sole*.

CHERRY, WILD OR CHOKE *Prunus virginiana* L.
Sturtevant, in *Notes on Edible Plants*, ed. U. P. Hedrick, says:

'Wood, in his New England Prospects, mentions choke cherries and says they are very austere and as yet "as wilde as Indians."'

CYTISSUS, SPANISH, SPANISH BROOM　　*Spartium junceum*
'They groweth naturally in many places of France, Spain and Italy, we have it as an ornament in our Gardens, among other delightful plants, to please the senses of sight and smelling.' Parkinson, *Paradisi*. 'It appears from Turner's Herbal that it was cultivated here in 1562 by Lord Cobham.' Miller.

DOGWOOD, FLOWERING　　*Cornus florida* L.
Native in North America. 'There is a variety of it with a rose-coloured involucre, which was found wild in Virginia by Banister, and afterwards by Catesby.' Miller. Introduced into England in 1739 by Philip Miller or perhaps earlier by Fairchild. Cultivated in Virginia between 1712 and 1719.

　　CORNELIAN CHERRY, CORNEL　　*Cornus mas* L.
'By reason of the pleasantnesse in them when they are ripe, they are much desired. They are also preserved and eaten.' Parkinson, *Paradisi*. 'Formerly it was cultivated for the fruit, which was used to make tarts, and a rob de Cornis was kept in the shops.' Miller.

　　RED OSIER　　*Cornus stolonifera* Michx.
　　SILKY DOGWOOD　　*Cornus amomum* Miller
Both valued for the red winter color of the young shoots.

FIR　　*Picea abies* L. Karsten
'The Firre tree groweth naturally higher than any other tree in these parts in Christendom where no Cedars grow, and even equalling or over-topping the Pine.' Parkinson, *Paradisi*.

GELDER OR GUELDER ROSE　　*Viburnum opulus* L. var.
　　　　　　　　　　　　　　　　　　　　　roseum L.
The sterile form 'is generally called Sambucus rosea: In English, The Elder Rose, and more commonly after the Dutch name, the Gelder Rose.' Parkinson, *Paradisi*.

HACKBERRY, COMMON　　*Celtis occidentalis* L.

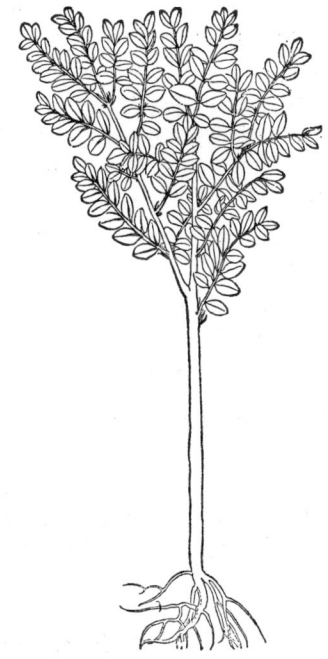

Boxwood, *Buxus*. From Fuchs, *De Historia stirpium*.

HEMLOCK *Tsuga canadensis* L. Carr.

HONEYSUCKLE, FRENCH, RED-SATIN FLOWERS
Lonicera periclymenum L.
L. caprifolium L.
HONEYSUCKLE, CORAL *Lonicera sempervirens* L.

HYPERICUM, ST. JOHN'S WORT *Hypericum perforatum* L.
'The common people in France and Germany gather it with great ceremony on St. John's day, and hang it in their windows, as a charm against storms, thunder, and evil spirits; mistaking the meaning of some medical writers, who have fancifully given this plant the name of *Fuga Daemonum*, from a supposition that it was good in maniacal and hypochondracal disorders.' Miller.

JASMINE *Jasminum officinale* L.
'Gerard cultivated this shrub in 1597. He says it was then common in most parts of England, being used for arbors and to cover banqueting houses in gardens.' Miller.

JASMINE, CAROLINA *Gelseminum sempervirens* L. Aiton fil.
'Groweth in Virginia as Master *Tradescant*, who saw it there doth affirme, and from him I have a plant risen of the seed. [It] was never mentioned by any before, and but that Master *Tradescant* is confident to call it a Jasmine, and therefore I am content to put it with the rest to give him content, I would be further informed of it my selfe, before I would certainly give it my consent.' Parkinson, *Theatrum*.

JUNIPER, SAVIN See SAVIN TREE OR BUSH

JUNIPER, RED CEDAR *Juniperus virginiana* L.
'This tree is much used for wanescotting rooms, making escritoirs, cabinets, etc., cockroches and other insects disliking the smell of it.' Miller.

LABURNUM *Laburnum anagyroides* Medic.
'There is no use hereof in Physick with us, nor in the natural place of the growing, save only to provoke a vomit, which it will do very strongly.' Parkinson, *Paradisi*.

LANTANA *Lantana camara* L.
Cultivated probably for summer bedding. It was cultivated in 1691 in the royal garden at Hampton Court.

LARCH *Larix decidua*, Miller
'The coles of the wood hereof (because it is so hard and durable as none more) is held to be of most force being fined, to cause the iron oare to melt, which none other would do so well.' Parkinson, *Paradisi*.

LILAC, PIPE TREE See SYRINGA

LINDEN, LIME *Tilia europaea* L.
Although a hybrid, it does produce some viable seed. Culti-

vated at least as early as 1562. 'The coles of the wood are the best to make gunpowder and being handled, and quenched in vinegar, are good to dissolve clotted blood in those that are bruised with a fall.' Parkinson, *Paradisi*. 'The most elegant use to which it is applied is for carving. Many of Gibbons's beautiful works in Lime tree are dispersed about the kingdom in our churches and palaces.' Miller.

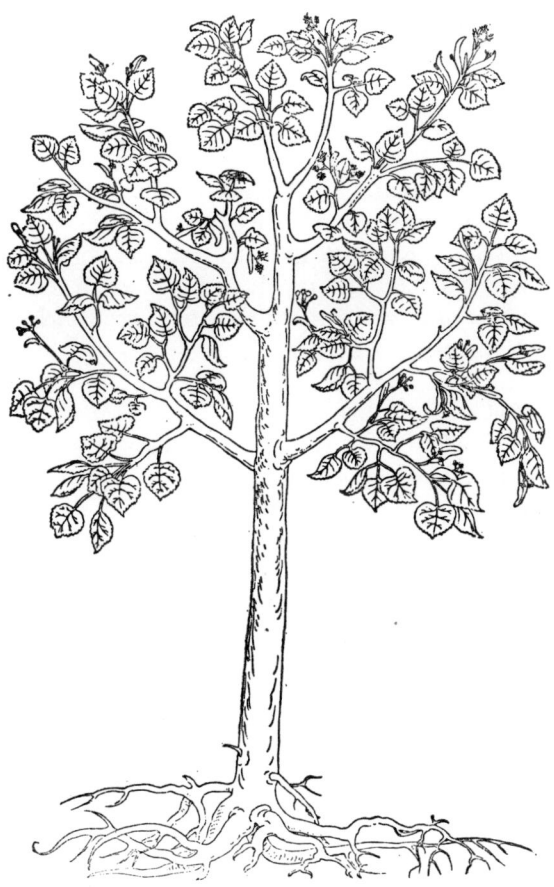

Linden tree, *Tilia foe*. From Fuchs, *De Historia stirpium*.

LOCUST   *Robinia pseudo-acacia* L.
'Native of North America, where it grows to a very large size, and the wood is much valued for its duration. Most of the houses which were built at Boston in New England, on the first settling of the English, were constructed of this timber.' Miller.

MAGNOLIA, SWEETBAY   *Magnolia virginiana* L.
'In America this tree is known by the names of White Laurel, Swamp Sassafras, and Beaver Tree. It has the last name, because the root is eaten as a great dainty by Beavers; and this animal is caught by means of it.' Miller.

MAPLE, RED   *Acer rubrum* L.
'This sort was cultivated in 1656 by Mr. John Tradescant, jun. . . . It is propagated with us for the sake of the scarlet flowers, which come out early in the spring. In Pennsylvania, where it grows in the swamps, the natives use it for almost all sorts of wood-work; with the bark they dye a dark blue, and make a good black ink.' Miller.

MEZEREUM (CHAMELAEA)   *Daphne mezereum* L.
Gerarde cultivated it in 1596. 'The branches make a good yellow dye. . . . The berries when swallowed prove a powerful poison. . . . There are two principal varieties of the Mezereum; one with a white flower succeeded by yellow berries; the other with peach-coloured flowers and red fruit; the latter has sometimes flowers of a much deeper red. There is also a variety with variegated leaves.' Miller.

MOCK ORANGE   *Philadelphus coronarius* L.
Lilacs, Mock Oranges, and some Jasmines were confused at this period. Mock Orange was *Syringa flore albo simplici* (Syringa with single white flowers), the single white pipe-tree. The double white pipe-tree or *Syringa Arabica flore albo duplici* (Syringa of Arabia with double flowers) is *Jasminum sambac* the Arabian Jasmine. The Lilacs were called *Lilac sive syringa*. Mock Orange was cultivated by Gerarde in 1596.

OAK, RED   *Quercus borealis* Michx. fil.
G. B. Emerson, in *Trees and Shrubs of Massachusetts*, says: 'The red oak is of little value for fuel or for most purposes as timber. ... But, like some individuals in a higher field in creation, it compensates in some measure for its comparative uselessness, by its great beauty.'

OAK, SCARLET   *Quercus coccinea* Muench.

OAK, WHITE   *Quercus alba* L.
'Acorns were dried and boiled for food by the Narragansetts. Oak acorns were mixed with their pottage by the Indians of Massachusetts. Baskets full of parched acorns, hid in the ground, were discovered by the Pilgrims December 7, 1620.' Sturtevant's *Notes*. It was not cultivated in England until 1724.

PERIPLOCA   *Asclepias syriaca* L.
Virgina silk, Wisanck Milkweed. 'I know not of any in our Land hath made any tryall of the properties hereof. Captain John Smith in his book of the discovery and description of Virginia, saith, that the Virginians use the roots hereof ... being bruised and applyed to cure their hurts and diseases.' Parkinson, *Paradisi*.

PHILADELPHUS   See MOCK ORANGE

PINE   *Pinus* sp.
It is likely that individual trees of various species were allowed to persist around the homesteads and in pastures.

PIPE TREE   See SYRINGA, MOCK ORANGE, or JASMINE

POPLAR   *Populus alba* or *P. nigra*
Both species were used at this period for timber.

PRIVET   *Ligustrum vulgare* L. and
                                var. *italicum* (Miller) Vahl
'In point of utility and ornament few shrubs exceed the com-

mon privet. Its chief use is to form such hedges as are required in dividing gardens for shelter or ornament, and for this the Italian or Evergreen Privet is usually preferred. It is one of the few plants that will thrive in the smoke of London.' Miller.

PYRACANTHA *Pyracantha* sp.
Cultivated by Parkinson in 1629. 'It is preferred with divers as an ornament to a garden or orchard, by reason of his ever green leaves, and red berries among them.' Parkinson, *Paradisi*.

RED-BUD   See ARBOR-JUDAE

ROSE *Rosa* sp. & cvs.
Many roses were cultivated, too many to deal with here. The reader should refer to Rose of Sharon—see Althea.

SAINT JOHN'S WERT   See HYPERICUM

SASSAFRAS *Sassafras albidum* (Nutt.) Nees.
'A decoction of Sassafras with sugar was sold in coffeehouses at the end of the last century, under the name of Bochet.' Miller.

SAVIN TREE OR BUSH, SAVINE *Juniperus sabina* L.
Cultivated in 1562 according to Turner. 'It is planted in out-yeards, bush-sides or void places of Orchards, as well, to cast cloaths thereon to dry, as for medicines both for men and horses: being made with an oyle, it is good to annoint children's bellies for to kill the worms.' Parkinson, *Paradisi*.

SERVICE TREE OR SORBUS *Sorbus torminalis* Crantz
'The fruit of this tree is in some round like an apple, and in others a little longer like a pear, but of a more pleasant taste than the ordinary kind, when they are ripe and mellowed, as they used to do both with these kinds and with Medlars.' Parkinson, *Paradisi*.

SMOKE TREE, VENICE SUMACKE *Cotinus coggygria* Scopoli
'The wood is yellowish, and serveth to give a yellow dye: but

the leaves and young branches, doe Dye a blacke colour; and with the barke they Tanne leather.' Parkinson, *Theatrum*.

SPICEBUSH *Lindera Benzoin* Blume
'Native of Virginia; whence it was sent by Banister to Compton Bishop of London, and cultivated in his garden at Fulham in 1688.' Miller.

SPIRAEA, SPIRAEA FRUTEX *Spiraea salicifolia* L.
'It appears from Rea's Flora that the common Spiraea Frutex was cultivated here in 1665.' Miller.

SWEET GUM *Liquidambar styraciflua* L.
Cultivated by Bishop Compton in 1688. 'From between the wood and the bark issues a fragrant gum, which trickles from the wounded trees, and by the heat of the sun congeals into transparent drops, which the Indians chew as a preservation to their teeth. . . . The Bark is also of singular use to the Indians for covering their huts.' Miller.

SYCAMORE *Platanus occidentalis* L.
Cultivated in England in 1640 by John Tradescant, Jr. 'The English Americans call it Button-wood . . . or Water Beech. . . . It grows mostly in low places. . . . It is easily transplanted to drier places, if the soil be good, . . . it is planted about houses and in gardens to afford a pleasant shade in the hot season.' Miller.

SYRINGA, PERSIAN *Syringa persica* L.
'It appears from the Catalogue of the Oxford garden that it was cultivated here in 1658.' Miller.

SYRINGA, PIPE TREE See also PHILADELPHUS
'Gerarde and Parkinson cultivated the blue and white Lilac under the name of Pipe Tree or Privets. The former says, "I have them growing in my garden in great plenty" 1597—Mattiolus's figure [1598?] is engraved from a drawing which was taken from a plant brought over from Constantinople by Augerius de Busbeke, who during seven years was Ambassador to

the Sultan Soliman from the Emperor Ferdinand I.' Miller.

TRUMPETCREEPER *Campsis radicans* Seem.
Cultivated in England in 1640. 'This never bore flower with mee, nor any other that hath it in our country that I could heare of: but in the naturall place, as also beyond the sea, at *Rome*, and other warme countries it beareth a great tuft of flowers together.' Parkinson, *Theatrum*.

TULIP TREE *Liriodendron tulipifera* L.
Cultivated by Bishop Compton at Fulham in 1688.

VIRGINIA CREEPER *Parthenocissus quinquefolia* (L.) Planch.
Cultivated by Parkinson in 1629.

WITCH-HAZEL *Hamamelis virginiana* L.
Native in Eastern North America. Introduced into England by Peter Collinson in 1736.

V Fruits and Nuts before 1700

ALMOND *Prunus dulcis* (P. Miller) D. A. Webb (*P. amygdalus* Batsch.)
Native in western Asia. Phillip Miller knew 3 varieties in 1743, The Common, the Sweet with Tender Shells, and the Bitter.

APPLE Hybrid derivations from *Malus pumila* Miller.
Native in Europe and western Asia. Apple seeds were introduced by the first Colonists, and gave rise to 'American' cultivars. Although the art of grafting was known, apples were commonly propagated by seed for the next two hundred years. The Hon. Paul Dudley of Roxbury, who was Chief Justice of Massachusetts, published in 1734 a paper in the Philosophical Transactions of the Royal Society of London entitled: 'Some Observations on the Plants of New England . . .' in which he comments, 'Our apples are without doubt as good as those of England, and much fairer to look to; . . . A good apple tree with us will measure from six to ten foot in girth.' Quoted in U. P. Hedrick, *A History of Horticulture in America*.

APRICOT, APRICOCK, ABRICOT *Prunus armeniaca* L.
Native in western Asia. As late as 1743 there were only about eight varieties of Apricot in cultivation in Great Britain.

BARBERRY *Berberis vulgaris* L.
Native in Europe. Philip Miller, in *The Gardener's Dictionary*,

says that it 'grows naturally in the hedges in many parts of England, but is also cultivated in gardens for its fruit, which is pickled and used for garnishing dishes. . . . The fruit is used for pickling and for preserving; a decoction of the berries sweetened is deemed useful as well as pleasant in fevers.'

CHERRIES, SOUR CHERRY *Prunus cerasus* L.
Native in southeastern Europe and western Asia. In *The Cherries of New York*, by Hedrick *et al.*, we read that 'Francis Higginson writing in 1629, after naming the several other fruits then under cultivation in Massachusetts, notes that the 'Red Kentish' is the only cherry cultivated. . . . As early as 1641, a nursery had been started in Massachusetts and was selling among other trees those of a cherry. . . . These early plantations of cherries in New England were undoubtedly grown from seed; . . . at least, the records make mention of seeds and not of trees.'

CURRANTS, RIBES *Ribes sylvestre* Mert. et Koch
Native in western Europe. 'There is little of interest or of profit to the pomologist in the history of the currant in America. The earliest English settlers in Massachusetts, . . . brought this fruit to the new country. Probably the sorts brought were the Red and White Dutch, and the fact that after those hundred years we still grow these varieties is significant, there have been few attempts to improve the currant in America.' Hedrick *et al.*, *The Small Fruits of New York*.

ELDERBERRY, ELDERN *Sambucus canadensis* L.
Native in eastern North America.

S. nigra L.
Native in Europe and western Asia. The berries were used for making wine and pies.

FIG *Ficus cariac* L.
Native in western Asia. 'In 1629 one Mistress Pearce, of Jamestown, an honest, industrious woman, had gathered from her garden in one year "neere an hundred bushels of excellent Figges."' Hedrick, *Small Fruits*.

FILBERT, FILBEARDS *Corylus avellana* L.
Native in Europe. P. Miller in 1743 recognized five sorts growing in England. European forms have not done well in this country except in the Northwest.

Currants, *Ribes*. From Fuchs, *De Historia stirpium*.

GOOSEBERRY *Ribes grossularia* L.
Native in Europe eastward to the Caucasus. 'The Gooseberry of history is well grown only in the Old World. Early settlers in America from England and Holland tried its culture here but the hot dry American summers parched and withered both fruit and foliage. Moreover, it was subject to a native mildew which, before preventive and remedial sprays were introduced, made short work of European Gooseberries in America. A few of the several hundred varieties grown in Europe vicariously grow in favored gardens in northeastern United States and adjacent parts of Canada.' Hedrick, *Small Fruits*.

GRAPES   *Vitis vinifera* L.
Probably native in the Caucasus. There were many attempts to grow foreign grapes in New England. John Winthrop, Governor of Massachusetts Bay Colony, had planted a vineyard in one of the islands, known as Governor's Garden, 'in Boston Harbor before 1630. Vine-planters were sent to this colony in 1629. There were plantations at the mouth of the Piscataqua in Maine as early or before Winthrop's plantings were made . . . if grapes were grown, or wine made from the foreign grape, no great degree of success was attained. Wine was made in plenty from the wild grapes in all of the New England colonies so that it was not because of Puritanical prejudices against wine that the grapes were not grown.' Hedrick *et al.*, *The Grapes of New York*.

HAWTHORN, OXYCANTHA   *Crataegus oxycanthoides* Thuill.
                                            C. monogyna Jacq.
Planted for hedges—a double-flowered cultivar was available for ornamental planting.

HAZELNUT, HAZEL   See FILBERTS

Hazel nuts, *Avellana nux*. From Fuchs, *De Historia stirpium*.

COLONIAL GARDENS

MEDLAR *Mespilus germanica* L.
Native from southeastern Europe to Persia. 'These fruits are permitted to remain upon the trees till *October*, when they will begin to fall; at which time they must be gathered when dry, and laid by in a dry place, until they become soft, and begin to decay, which is commonly about a Month after they are gathered, when they will be fit to be eaten; before which they are so very harsh, that it is almost impossible to eat them.' Miller P., *Gardener's Dictionary* Ed. 4, 1743.

MULBERRY *Morus nigra* L.
'Is very common in most gardens, being raised for the Delicacy of its fruit... *Morus alba* L. is commonly cultivated for its leaves to feed silk-worms.' Miller.

NECTARINE *Prunus persica* (L.) Batsch. var. *nectarina* (Aiton) Maxim.
John Parkinson, in *Paradisi in sole*, writes that 'they have been with us not many years. . . . We at this day doe know five several sorts.'

ORANGE, SEVILLE OR SOUR ORANGE *Citrus aurantium* L.
Native in southern Asia. First plantings in South Carolina made before 1577.'It is well known that oranges in small quantities have been grown for many years in South Carolina and Georgia, particularly on certain islands adjacent to the coast. It is therefore interesting to know that Bartholomé Martínez in a letter to the King dated at Havana, February 17, 1577, stated:"And what may be truthfully told to your Majesty is that in Santa Elena [Parris Island, South Carolina] I planted with my own hands grape vines, pomegranate trees, orange and fig trees; wheat, barley, onions, and garlic." Martínez had lived in Santa Elena until 1576. His garden therefore was planted before 1577, the date of his statement.

'It is clear from this evidence that citrus fruits were introduced into several sections of the southeastern United States in the latter part of the sixteenth century.' (Webber, H. J. & Batchelor, L. D., *The Citrus Industry*.)

PEACH   *Prunus persica* L.

'Of peaches in the New England colonies, we need say but little. Except in favored parts of Connecticut and Massachusetts, this fruit was little grown in these northern colonies. It is not at all probable that New England Indians ever planted peaches and for a generation after the whites came the struggle for the necessities of life kept them from indulging in so great a luxury as a peach-orchard. Strong drink was commonly used by the Puritans as by the Churchmen in Virginia and peach-brandy would have been as acceptable but it was easier to produce cider, and rum from the West Indies could be had with little trouble. Still, peaches were sparingly grown in the New England colonies.

'The Massachusetts Company in 1629 sent peach-pits, along with seeds of other fruits, to be planted by the colonists. Twelve years later George Fenwick, Saybrook, Connecticut, writes to Governor Winthrop that he is "prettie well storred with chirrie & peach trees." Justice Paul Dudley, who seems to have been the leading horticulturist in Massachusetts in his time, writes in 1726: "Our Peaches do rather excel those of England, and then we have not the Trouble or Expence of Walls for them; for our Peach Trees are all standards and I have had in my own Garden seven or eight Hundred fine Peaches of the Rare-ripes, growing at a Time on one Tree." From another statement made by Justice Dudley we learn that peaches were still being grown from the stone and may assume that budding was not known, or so careful a horticulturist as our author would have mentioned it. He says: "Our Peach Trees are large and fruitful, and bear commonly in three Years from the Stone. I have one in my Garden of twelve years growth, that measures two Foot and an Inch in Girt a Yard from the ground which, two Years ago, bore me near a Bushel of fine Peaches."' Hedrick *et al.*, *The Peaches of New York*.

'In the voyages undertaken for exploration and commerce soon after the discovery of America by Columbus the peach was introduced in America by the Spanish; for soon after permanent settlement had been made in the South the settlers found this fruit in widespread cultivation by the Indians and its origin could only be traced to the Spaniards who early visited Florida and the Gulf region. William Penn wrote as early as 1683 that there were very good peaches in Pennsylvania; "not an Indian plantation was without them." The abundance of this fruit was noted by all the early travelers in the region from Pennsylvania southward and westward.' Hedrick *et al.*, *The Plums of New York*.

Peach tree, *Persica*. From Fuchs, *De Historia stirpium*.

PEAR, PEARE   *Pyrus communis* L.
Native in Europe and western Asia. 'He [Justice Dudley] says: "An *Orange* Pear Tree grows the largest and yields the fairest Fruit. I know one of them near forty Foot high, that measures six Foot and six Inches in Girt, a Yard from the Ground, and has borne thirty Bushels at a Time: and this year I measured an Orange Pear, that grew in my own Orchard, of eleven Inches round the Bulge. I have a Warden Pear Tree, that measures five Foot six Inches round. One of my Neighbors has a Bergamot Pear Tree that was brought from England in a Box, about the Year 1643, that now measures six Foot about, and has borne twenty-two Bushels of fine Pears in one Year. About twenty years since, the Owner took a Cyon, and grafted it upon a common Hedge Pear; but the Fruit does not prove altogether so good, and the Rind or Skin, is thicker than that of the Original.' Hedrick *et al.*, *The Pears of New York*.

PLUM   *Prunus domestica* L.
Native in Europe and western Asia. 'In Massachusetts some plums were planted by the Pilgrims, for Francis Higginson, writing in 1629, says: "Our Governor hath already planted a vineyard with great hope of increase. Also mulberries, plums, raspberries, corrance, chestnuts, filberts, walnuts, smalnuts, hurtleberries." The plums were Damsons, as a statement is made a little later that the "Red Kentish is the only cherry and the Damson the only plum cultivated." A further reference to this plum is made by John Josselyn, when, writing of a voyage to New England in 1663, he says, "The Quinces, Cherries, Damsons, set the dames a work, marmalad and preserved Damsons is to be met with in every house."

'In 1797 there is the following concise account of the plums cultivated in New England.

' "The better sorts which are cultivated are the horse plum, a very pleasant tasted fruit, of large size; the peach plum, red toward the sun, with an agreeable tartness; the pear plum, so-called from its shape, which is sweet, and of an excellent taste; the wheat plum, extremely sweet, oval, and furrowed in the middle, not large; the green-gage plum, which is generally preferred before all the rest." ' Hendrick, *The Plums*.

POMEGRANATE *Punica granatum* L.
Native from southeastern Europe to the Himalayas. Pomegranates do not survive outdoors north of Washington. The first greenhouse in New England seems to have been that of Andrew Faneuil in the early 1700's, so it is unlikely that any planting of pomegranate in this area before that was successful. However, two or three varieties were known in England, so it is likely that some colonists may have tried to raise plants from seed.

QUINCE *Cydonia oblonga* Miller
Native in central Asia. John Josselyn, in *New England Rarities*, writes: 'Our fruit-trees prosper abundantly, *Apple-trees*, *Pear-trees*, *Quince-trees*, *Cherry-trees*, *Plum-trees*, *Barberry-trees*. I have observed with admiration that the Kernels sown or succors planted produce as fair and good fruit without grafting as the Tree from whence they were taken.'

RASPBERRIES *Rubus idaeus* L.
Native through much of the North Temperate Zone. 'The Raspis berries is of two sorts, white and red, not differing in the form either of bush, leafe or berry, but onely in the colour and taste of the fruit.' Parkinson, *Paradisi*.

STRAWBERRIES *Fragaria virginiana* Duchesne
The common native strawberry was mentioned by the early European explorers and pioneers on our Atlantic seaboard. *Fragaria chiloensis*, one of the parents of the modern cultivated strawberries did not arrive in Europe from Chile until 1712.

WALNUTS *Juglans regina* L.
Native from southeastern Europe to China. 'As there do not perhaps exist . . . , south of the Hudson river, ten European Walnut trees . . .' *Juglans nigra* L. 'These nuts are sold in the Markets of New York, Philadelphia, and Baltimore, and served upon the tables.' Hillhouse, S. L. (Trans.) Michaux, F. A. *The North American Sylva*. 3 vols. Paris. C. D'Hautel. 1819.

VI Flowers, 1700 to 1776

ASTER, CHINA *Callistephus chinensis* (L.) Nees.
Native in China and Japan. Sent by French missionaries to Paris, grown in England about 1731.

ASTER, STOKES *Stokesia laevis* (Hill) Greene
Native in North America from South Carolina to Louisiana. Introduced to England by James Gordon about 1766.

BALSAM, DOUBLE *Impatiens balsamina* L.
Double-flowered forms were not known in 1640 but were so common as not to be of exceptional note in 1759.

BEARBERRY *Arctostaphyllos uva-ursi* L.
Native in the Northern Hemisphere. Discovered in Britain before 1700 and noted in America by Kalm in 1750.

BEDSTRAW, YELLOW *Galium varum* L.
Native throughout Europe. Cultivated in England in 1597.

BEE BALM *Monarda didyma* L.
Native from New York to Michigan, south to Georgia and Tennessee. Cultivated in England by Peter Collinson in 1755.

BENT GRASS *Agrostis tenuis* Sibthorp
(and perhaps other species)
Native in Europe. Long cultivated in pastures.

BLACK-EYED SUSAN *Rudbeckia hirta* L.
Native in North America from western Massachusetts to Illinois, south to Georgia and Alabama. Cultivated in Britain in 1732 by James Sherard.

BOUNCING BET, SOAPWORT *Saponaria officinalis* L.
Native in Europe. Long cultivated.

CARNATION, CLOVE PINK *Dianthus caryophyllus* L.
Native in southern Europe. Cultivated in England in 1597.

CATCHFLY, MORNING CAMPION, RED CAMPION
Melandrium rubrum (Weigel)
Garcke (*Lychnis dioica* L.)
Native in Europe, western Asia, and North Africa. Cultivated in Britain in 1633.

CATCHFLY *Viscaria vulgaris* Bernh.
(*Lychnis viscaria* L.)
Native in Europe and western Asia. Cultivated in Britain in 1644.

CAT-TAIL *Typha latifolia* L.
Widespread in the northern Hemisphere. Long used in rural crafts.

COCKSCOMB *Celosia argentea* L. var.
cristata (L.) Kuntz
Native in the Asiatic tropics. Cultivated in Britain in 1597.

COLUMBINE *Aquilegia canadensis* L.
Native in North America from Newfoundland to Wisconsin, south to Georgia and Tennessee. Cultivated in England before 1640 by John Tradescant, Sr.

COREOPSIS, TICKSEED *Coreopsis lanceolata* L.
Native in North America from Virginia to Wisconsin, south to Florida and New Mexico. Cultivated in Britain in 1725

CREEPING JENNY, CREEPING CHARLEY, MONEYWORT
Lysimachia nummularia L.
Native in Europe and Asia. Cultivated in England in 1597.

EVENING PRIMROSE *Oenothera biennis* L.
Native throughout the United States. Originally cultivated at Padua in 1619 and in England in 1629.

FALL DAFFODIL *Sternbergia lutea* (L.) J. A. and J. H. Schult.
Native in southern Europe. Cultivated in England in 1597.

FOAMFLOWER *Tiarella cordifolia* L.
Native from New Brunswick to Michigan, south to North Carolina and Tennessee. Cultivated in Britain in 1731.

GALAX *Galax aphylla* L.
Native from Virginia and West Virginia, south to Georgia and Alabama. Cultivated in Britain in 1751.

GOLDEN RAGWORT *Senecio aureus* L.
Native from Maryland to Missouri, south to Florida and Arkansas. Cultivated in England in 1759.

HYDRANGEA *Hydrangea arborescens* L.
Native from New York to Missouri, south to Georgia and Oklahoma. Cultivated in England in 1736 by Peter Collinson.

INKBERRY *Ilex glabra* (L.) Gray
Native from Nova Scotia to Florida and Louisiana. Cultivated in Britain in 1759.

IRIS, DWARF *Iris pumila* L.
Native from central Europe to Asia Minor. Cultivated in Britain in 1596.

LIZARD'S TAIL *Saururus cernuus* L.
Native from Rhode Island and Quebec to Kansas, south to Florida and Texas. Cultivated in England in 1759.

LUNARIA, MOONWORT, HONESTY *Lunaria annua* L.
Native in southeastern Europe. Cultivated in Britain in 1596.

MAIDENHAIR FERN *Adiantum pedatum* L.
Native from Quebec and Minnesota, south to Georgia and Louisiana. Cultivated in England by John Tradescant the younger before 1640.

MALLOW, ROSE *Hibiscus moscheutos* L.
Native from Maryland to Indiana, south to Florida and Alabama. Introduced to the Jardin des Plantes in Paris in 1644.

MEADOW RUE *Thalictrum aquilegifolium* L.
Native in Europe and Asia. Cultivated in England in 1731.

PEA, BEACH *Lathyrus japonicus* Willd. var. *glaber* (Ser.) Fernald (*Pisum maritimum* L. in part)
Native from Labrador to New Jersey, inland to the Great Lakes.

PERIWINKLE *Vinca minor* L.
Native in Europe. Long cultivated.

PHLOX *Phlox paniculata* L.
Native from New York to Iowa, south to Georgia and Arkansas. Cultivated in England in 1732 by James Sherard.
Phlox maculata L.
Native from Quebec to Minnesota, south to Tennessee and Missouri. Cultivated in England in 1759.
Phlox carolina L.
Native from Maryland to Indiana, south to North Carolina and Alabama. Cultivated in Britain before 1728.

PINKS, GRASS *Dianthus plumarius* L.
Native in southeastern Europe. Cultivated in Britain in 1629.

POPPY, ORIENTAL *Papaver orientale* L.
Native in the eastern Mediterranean region. Cultivated at Paris about 1700 and in England before 1714.

Poppy, Prickly *Argemone mexicana* L.
Native in the American tropics. Cultivated in Britain in 1592.

Snowdrop *Galanthus nivalis* L.
Native in central, southern, and eastern Europe. Long cultivated.

Sweet Pea, Annual *Lathyrus odoratus* L.
Native in Italy. Cultivated in Britain in 1700.

Trollius *Trollius europeus* L.
Native of Europe. Cultivated in England in 1581.

Turtlehead *Chelone glabra* L.
Native from Newfoundland to Minnesota, south to Georgia, Alabama and Missouri. Cultivated in Britain in 1730.
Chelone obliqua L.
Native from Maryland and Tennessee, south to Florida and Mississippi. Cultivated in Britain 1732.

Veronica *Veronica maritima* L.
Native in central Europe and northern Asia. Cultivated in England by Mr. Hugh Morgan in 1570.

Virginia Bluebells *Mertensia virginica* (L.) Pers.
Native from New York to Minnesota, south to South Carolina and Arkansas. Cultivated in England in 1699.

Whitlow Grass *Draba verna* L.
Native in Europe, Asia and North Africa. Long common as a garden weed.

VII Vegetables, 1700 to 1776

BROCCOLI *Brassica oleracea* L. var. *botrytis* L.
Native in Europe. Apparently originating in England (Europe?) sometime after 1680.

CAYENNE PEPPER *Capsicum frutescens* L. var. *longum* Bailey
Probably native in tropical America. Cultivated in England in 1656 by John Tradescant, Jr.

CELERY *Apium graveolens* L. var. *dulce* (Miller) Persoon
Native in Europe. Apparently celery was not developed until after 1640.

COTTON *Gossypium herbaceum* L.
Cultivated in Virginia as early as 1621, but not an important crop until much later.

LENTILS *Lens culinarius* Medic.
Native in southern Europe.

OKRA *Hibiscus esculentus* L.
Native in the Old World Tropics, cultivated in Britain in 1692.

PEAS, BLACK EYED OR COW PEAS *Vigna sinensis* (L.) Savi
Native in the Old World Tropics. Introduced in 1776.

Pepper Grass, Garden Cress   *Lepidium sativum* L.
Native in western Asia. Long cultivated.

Pepper, Guinea   See Cayenne Pepper

Rape   *Brassica napus* L.
Known only in cultivation. Long cultivated.

Scurvy Grass   *Cochlearia officinalis* L.
Native throughout the Artic and boreal regions. Long known as an antiscorbutic.

Sorrel, Garden   *Rumex acetosa* L.
Native in Europe and America. Long known as a salad herb.

Vetch, Tares   *Vicia sativa* L.
Native in Europe and Asia. Long cultivated as a stock food.

Yams   *Dioscorea alata* L.
Native from India to Malaya. Long cultivated in the tropics.

Strawberries, *Fragaria major*. From Fuchs, *De Historia stirpium*.

VIII Shrubs, Trees and Vines, 1700 to 1776

ACACIA, EGYPTIAN *Acacia farnesiana* (L.) Willd.
Probably native in Mexico or the West Indies, but now extensively naturalized in tropical areas. First cultivated in the garden of Cardinal Alessandro Farnese (The Farnese Palace) in 1611.

ALDER *Alnus glutinosa* (L.) Gaertn.
Native in Eurasia.

AMORPHA, BASTARD INDIGO *Amorpha fruticosa* L.
Native in eastern North America from southern Pennsylvania to Florida, west to Louisiana and Kansas. Sent to England by Mark Catesby in 1724.

ANDROMEDA *Leucothoe racemosa* (L.) Gray
Native in eastern North America from Massachusetts to Florida. Noted by Peter Kalm in 1750, but previously cultivated by Peter Collinson in England in 1736.

ARALIA OR DEVIL'S WALKING STICK *Aralia spinosa* L.
Native in North America from New Jersey to Iowa, south to Florida and Texas. Sent by Rev. John Banister from Virginia to Bishop Compton in England and cultivated by him in 1688.

ARROW-WOOD *Viburnum dentatum* L.
Native of North America from Massachusetts south to Florida and Texas. Cultivated in England by Peter Collinson in 1736.

Ash, American or White　　　　　*Fraxinus americana* L.
Native in North America from Quebec and Minnesota to Florida and Texas. Raised in England from seeds sent from New England in 1724 by Mr. Moore [? Robert More of Shrewsbury].

Ash, European　　　　　　　　　*Fraxinus excelsior* L.
Native in Europe. Cultivated in Britain for timber and fuel.

Azalea, Flame　　　　　　　　　*Rhododendron* sp.
Azaleas of the section Pentanthera which are native in eastern North America seem to have been much confused at this period.
Rhododendron calendulaceum (Michx.) Torr. was the most desired, with its deep red flowers, but *R. periclymenoides* (Michx.) Shinners (*R. nudiflorum*), *R. prionophyllum* (Small) Millais (*R. roseum*), *R. canescens* (Michx.) Sweet, and *R. atlanticum* (Ashe) Rehder seem all to have been cultivated. One or more was cultivated in England by Peter Collinson in 1734. *R. calendulaceum* was not surely known in cultivation before 1806.

Azalea, Indica　　　　　　　　　*Rhododendron indicum* Sweet
Known, but not cultivated in England in 1759; not surely introduced to cultivation in England until 1808. Probably introduced to Charleston, S.C., by André Michaux between 1787 and 1796.

Azaleas, Swamp White.　　　　　*Rhododendron viscosum*
　　　　　　　　　　　　　　　　　　　　　(L.) Torrey
Native in eastern North America from Maine to Tennessee. Cultivated in England in 1734 by Peter Collinson.

Beautyberry, American　　　　　*Callicarpa americana* L.
Native in North America from Maryland south to Florida and Texas. Sent by Mark Catesby from South Carolina to Philip Miller in England in 1724.

Beech, American　　　　　　　　*Fagus grandifolia* Ehrh.
Native in eastern North America from Prince Edward Island and Ontario to Florida and Texas. Introduced into cultivation in England in 1766 by the nursery firm of Kennedy and Lee.

BEECH, EUROPEAN *Fagus sylvatica* L.
Native in Europe. Used and cultivated for timber and food.

BIRCH, BLACK *Betula lenta* L.
Native in eastern North America from Maine to Georgia. Cultivated in England by Philip Miller in 1759.

BIRCH, RIVER *Betula nigra* L.
Native in eastern North America from southern New England to Florida and Texas. Cultivated in England by Peter Collinson in 1736.

BITTERSWEET, AMERICAN *Celastrus scandens* L.
Native in eastern North America from Quebec and Manitoba south to Georgia and Louisiana. Cultivated in England in 1736 by Peter Collinson.

BLACK GUM, TUPELO, BLACK TUPELO, SOUR GUM
Nyssa sylvatica Marshall
Native in eastern North America from Maine to Florida, Texas and Mexico. It was cultivated in Britain in 1750 by Archibald, Duke of Argyle.

BROOM, SCOTCH *Cytisus scoparius* (L.) Wimmer
Native in Europe, long known and cultivated for a variety of purposes.

BUCKEYE, SWEET *Aesculus octandra* Marshall
Native in eastern North America, from Pennsylvania and Iowa south to Georgia. Cultivated in England in 1764 by Mr. John Greening.

BURNING BUSH *Euonymus atropurpureus*, Jacq.
Native in eastern North America from Ontario and Montana south to Alabama. Cultivated in England in 1756 by Messrs. Lee and Kennedy.

BUTCHERS BROOM *Ruscus aculeatus* L.
Native in southern Europe.

BUTTERNUT *Juglans cinerea* L.
Native in eastern North America from New Brunswick to North Dakota and south to Georgia. Cultivated in England by John Tradescant, Jr., in 1656.

BUTTON BUSH *Cephalanthus occidentalis* L.
Native in eastern North America from Nova Scotia to Florida and Mexico. Cultivated in England in 1735 by Peter Collinson.

CAROLINA ALLSPICE, SWEETSHRUB *Calycanthus floridus* L.
Native in eastern North America from Pennsylvania and Ohio to Florida and Mississippi. Introduced into cultivation in England by Mark Catesby in 1726.

CASSINE, CASSIOBERRY, YAUPON *Ilex vomitoria* Aiton
Ilex cassine L.
Native of eastern North America, from southeastern Virginia south to Florida and Texas. Cultivated in England before 1700. Cassioberry is more properly a common name of *Ilex cassine* L. It is native on the coastal plains from North Carolina to Florida and Louisiana. Seed was sent to England in 1726 by Mark Catesby.

CATALPA, SOUTHERN CATALPA *Catalpa bignonioides* Walter
Native from Georgia and Florida to Mississippi. Sent to England by Mark Catesby in 1726.

CEDAR, ATLANTIC WHITE *Chamaecyparis thyoides* (L.) BSP.
Native in eastern North America from Maine to Florida and Mississippi. Cultivated in England by Peter Collinson about 1736.

CHASTE TREE *Vitex agnus-castus* L.
Native in southern Europe and Western Asia. Cultivated in England in 1570 and recorded in Virginia by 1762.

CHERRY LAUREL *Prunus caroliniana* (Miller) Aiton
Native from South Carolina to Texas. Introduced into Eng-

land about 1750 by Philip Miller. Probably introduced to cultivation in Charleston by Mark Catesby about 1725.

CHINA-BERRY, FRUIT OF CHINA, BEAD TREE
Melia azedarach L.
Native in southern Asia. Cultivated in England in 1656. Said to have been introduced to Charleston, S.C., by André Michaux between 1787 and 1796.

CHINQUAPIN *Castanea pumila* (L.) Miller
Native in eastern North America from Massachusetts to Florida and Texas. Cultivated in England in 1699 by the Duchess of Beaufort.

CHOKEBERRY, RED *Aronia arbutifolia* (L.) Ell.
Native in eastern North America, from Nova Scotia to Texas. Mentioned by Josselyn in 1673 and cultivated in England by the Earl of Clarendon in 1700.

CLEMATIS, VIRGIN'S BOWER *Clematis virginiana* L.
Native from the Gaspé Peninsula to Manitoba and south to Georgia and Louisiana. Cultivated in England in 1767 by James Gordon.

CLETHRA, SWEET PEPPER BUSH *Clethra alnifolia* L.
Native in eastern North America from Maine south to Florida and Texas. Introduced into cultivation in England about 1730.

COFFEE-BEAN, KENTUCKY OR KENTUCKY COFFEE TREE
Gymnocladus dioica (L.) K. Koch
Native in North America from central New York to South Dakota, south to Tennessee and Oklahoma. First cultivated in Europe at Paris, cultivated in England by Archibald, Duke of Argyle in 1748.

CORALBERRY *Symphoricarpos orbiculatus* Moench.
Native in North America from Pennsylvania to Colorado, south to Florida and Texas. Cultivated in England in 1730.

CORNEL, WHITE *Cornus alba* L.
Native in northeastern Asia. Cultivated in England by Philip Miller in 1759.

COWBERRY OR LINGON *Vaccinium vitis-idaea* L.
This is the common name of the plant which has probably never been cultivated in this country.

CRANBERRY *Vaccinium oxycoccus* L.
This fruit was much esteemed in the Philadelphia market at the time of Kalm's visit. Not cultivated, however, until 1802.

CRABAPPLE, WILD SWEET CRABAPPLE, ANCHOR TREE
Malus coronaria (L.) Miller
Native in North America from New York to Wisconsin and south to Tennessee. Cultivated in England in 1724.

CRAPE-MYRTLE, COMMON *Lagerstroemia indica* L.
Native in China. First introduced into Europe in 1747. Cultivated in England in 1759 by Hugh, Duke of Northumberland. Introduced to Charleston by André Michaux between 1787 and 1796.

CROSS-VINE *Bignonia capreolata* L.
Native in eastern north America from Maryland to Illinois south to Florida and Louisiana. Cultivated in England in 1730.

CYPRESS, BALD OR DECIDUOUS *Taxodium distichum* (L.) Richard
Native in North America from New Jersey to Illinois, south to Florida and Texas. Cultivated in England in 1640 by John Tradescant, Sr.

CYRILLA, SWAMP *Cyrilla racemiflora* L.
Native in eastern North America from Virginia to Florida and Texas. Cultivated in England in 1765 by John Cree.

ELDER, AMERICAN *Sambucus canadensis* L.
Native in eastern North America from Cape Breton Island and

Manitoba to Georgia and Louisiana. Cultivated in England in 1768.

ELDER, BOX *Acer negundo* L.
Native in North America from western New England and Minnesota south to Florida and Texas. Cultivated in England by Bishop Compton in 1688.

ELM, AMERICAN *Ulmus americana* L.
Native in North America from the Gaspé to Saskatchewan, south to Florida and Texas. Introduced into cultivation in England in 1752.

ELM, WINGED *Ulmus alata* Michx.
Native in North America from Virginia west to Illinois, southward to Florida and Texas. Possibly cultivated here, but not introduced to England until 1820.

EMERUS *Coronilla emerus* L.
Native. Cultivated in England in the time of Gerarde, 1596.

FERN, SWEET *Comptonia peregrina* (L.) Coulter
Native in North America from Cape Breton Island to Manitoba, south to Georgia and Tennessee. Cultivated in England in 1714 by the Duchess of Beaufort.

FLOWERING ALMOND, DWARF *Prunus glandulosa* Thunberg var. *sinensis* (Persoon) Koehne fil.
Native in east Asia. Introduced into cultivation in England in 1687 according to Rehder.

FOTHERGILLA, DWARF *Fothergilla gardenii* Murr.
Native from North Carolina to Florida and Alabama. Cultivated in England in 1765.

FRANKLINIA *Franklinia alatamaha* Marshall
Discovered in Georgia in 1765. It was grown by John Bartram

in his botanical garden, but not used extensively in garden plantings at this period.

FRINGE TREE *Chionanthus virginica* L.
Native in North America from New Jersey and Ohio south to Florida and Texas. Cultivated in England in 1736 by Peter Collinson.

GOLDEN RAIN TREE *Koelreuteria paniculata,* Laxmann
Native in China, Korea, and Japan. Cultivated in England in 1763.

GRAPE, MUSCADINE, SCUPPERNONG *Vitis rotundifolia* Michx.
Not surely cultivated before 1850 but the fruit likely collected from the wild throughout the period.

GROUNDSEL TREE *Baccharus halimifolia* L.
Native in North America from Massachusetts south to Florida, Texas, and Mexico. Cultivated in England in 1688 by Bishop Compton.

HAW, BLACK, OR BLACKHAW VIBURNUM
Viburnum prunifolium L.
Native in North America from Connecticut and Kansas, south to Florida and Texas. Cultivated in England in 1731.

HAWTHORN, COCK-SPUR OR HAW *Crataegus crus-galli* L.
Native in North America from southeastern Canada west to Minnesota, south to South Carolina and Texas. Cultivated in England in 1691 by the Honorable Charles Howard.

HAWTHORN, OR MAY *Crataegus oxycantha* L.
Native in Europe and North Africa. Long cultivated.

HAWTHORN, WASHINGTON THORN
Crataegus phaenopyrum (L.f.) Medic.
Native in North America from Pennsylvania and Missouri to Florida. Cultivated in England in 1738.

COLONIAL GARDENS 131

HICKORY, SCALY-BARK *Carya ovata* (Miller) K. Koch
Native in North America from Maine to Nebraska south to Florida and Texas. Cultivated in 1629.

HICKORY, SHELLBARK *Carya laciniosa* Loud.
Native from New York to Nebraska, south to Alabama and Louisiana. Not surely cultivated before 1804.

HOLLY, EVERGREEN *Ilex aquifolium* L.
Ilex opaca Aiton
The European Holly was repeatedly imported to America but with little success. American Holly was cultivated in England by 1744.

HOLLY, SWAMP OR POSSUM HAW *Ilex decidua* Walter
Native in North America from Maryland and Kansas south to Florida and Texas. Cultivated in Britain in 1760 by Archibald, Duke of Argyle.

HONEY LOCUST *Gleditsia triacanthos* L.
Native in North America from New York and South Dakota to Florida and Texas. Cultivated in England in 1700 by Bishop Compton.

HONEYSUCKLE, TARTARIAN *Lonicera tatarica* L.
Native in Southern Russia. Cultivated in England in 1752.
 HONEYSUCKLE, WILD OR PINXTERBLOOM AZALEA
  See AZALEA, FLAME

HORNBEAM, AMERICAN *Carpinus caroliniana* Walter
Native from Nova Scotia to Minnesota, south to Florida and Texas. Not introduced into England until 1812.

HORSE CHESTNUT *Aesculus hippocastanum* L.
Philip Miller, in *The Gardener's Dictionary*, says: 'The Horse-chestnut was brought from the northern part of Asia into Europe about the year 1550, and was sent to Vienna about the year 1558. From Vienna it migrated into Italy and France: but it came to us from the Levant immediately. Gerard, in his

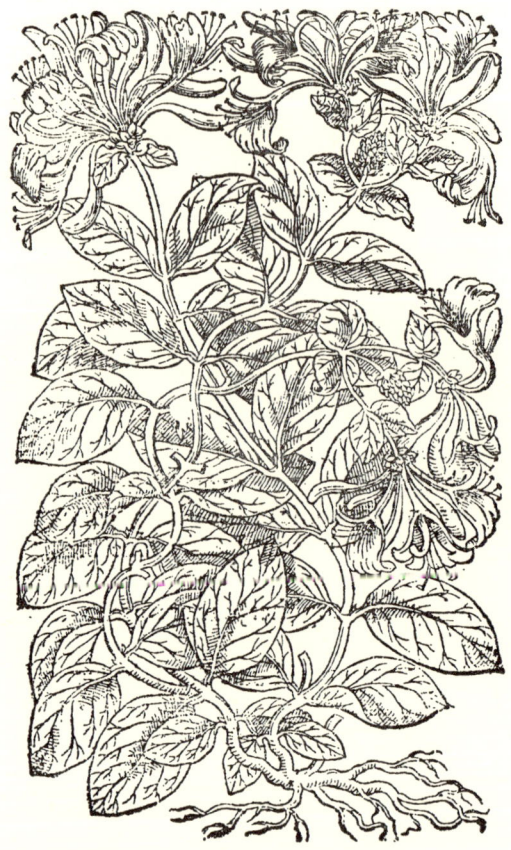

Honeysuckle, *Periclymenum*. From Gerarde, *Herball*.

herbal, speaks of it only as a foreign tree. In Johnson's edition of the same work, it is said, "Horse-chestnut groweth in Italy-and in sundry dry places of the East Countries; it is now growing with Mr. Tradescant at South-Lambeth." Parkinson says, "our Christian world had first the knowledge of it from Constantinople." ' Introduced to Philadelphia by John Bartram in 1746.

COLONIAL GARDENS 133

HORSE CHESTNUT, DWARF; RED BUCKEYE
Aesculus pavia L.
Native in North America from Virginia south to Florida and Louisiana. Cultivated in England in 1712.

HYDRANGEA, SMOOTH   *Hydrangea arborescens* L.
Native in eastern North America from southwestern New York to Missouri, southward to Florida and Louisiana. Cultivated in England in 1736 by Peter Collinson.

INKBERRY   *Ilex glabra* (L.) Gray
Native in eastern North America from Nova Scotia to Florida. Cultivated in England in 1759.

IRONWOOD OR HOP TREE   *Ostrya virginiana* (Miller) K. Koch
Native from Nova Scotia to Manitoba, south to Georgia and Oklahoma. Cultivated in England in 1692.

IVY, ENGLISH   *Hedera helix* L.
Native in Europe. Cultivated from ancient times. Reported in cultivation in North America by Kalm in 1750.

JUNIPER   *Juniperus communis* L.
Native in Eurasia and North America. Cultivated in England in 1560.

JUNIPER, CHINESE   *Juniperus chinensis* L.
Native in China, Mongolia and Japan. Cultivated in England by 1767.

LAUREL, OR IVY, OR MOUNTAIN LAUREL   *Kalmia latifolia* L.
Native from New Brunswick to Ohio, south to Florida and Louisiana. Introduced to England by Peter Collinson in 1734.
Rhododendron maximum L.
Native from Nova Scotia to Ohio, south to Georgia and Alabama. Introduced to England in 1736 by Peter Collinson. It did not flower there until 1756.

LEATHERWOOD *Dirca palustris* L.
Native from New Brunswick to Minnesota, south to Florida and Louisiana. Introduced in Britian by Archibald, Duke of Argyle, in 1750.

LEUCOTHOE *Leucothoe axillaris* (Lam.) D. Don
Native in eastern North America from Virginia to Florida and Mississippi. Cultivated in England in 1765 by John Cree.

LINDEN, AMERICAN *Tilia americana* L.
Native from New Brunswick to Manitoba south to Alabama and Texas. Cultivated in England in 1752.

LOBLOLLY PINE *Pinus taeda* L.
Native in eastern North America from New Jersey to Texas. Cultivated in England in 1736.

LOCUST, PINK OR ROSE ACACIA LOCUST *Robinia hispida* L.
Native from Virginia and Tennessee southward. Cultivated in England in 1758.

MAGNOLIA, SOUTHERN OR CAROLINA LAUREL
Magnolia grandiflora L.
Native in eastern North America from North Carolina to Texas. Sent to England before 1737 by Mark Catesby.

MAPLE, NORWAY *Acer platanoides* L.
Native in Europe. Not cultivated in England until 1724. Introduced by William Hamilton of Philadelphia after the Revolutionary War.

MAPLE, SILVER *Acer saccharinum* L.
Native in North America from New Brunswick to Minnesota southward. At this period much confused with Sugar Maple. Said to have been introduced in England in 1725.

MAPLE, SUGAR *Acer saccharum* Marshall
Native in North America from the Gaspé to Manitoba, south

COLONIAL GARDENS

to Georgia and Texas. Silver and Sugar Maple were distinguished by Humphrey Marshall in 1785. Said to have been cultivated in England in 1735.

MESPILUS, SNOWY *Amelanchier stolonifera* Weigand

Native in eastern North America from Newfoundland to Ontario, south to Virginia. Judging by the description of cultivated plants, this probably was the species cultivated in England as early as 1746.

MIMOSA *Albizia julibrissin* Dur.

Native from Persia to China. Cultivated in England in 1745.

MOOSEWOOD *Acer pensylvanicum* L.

Native from Quebec to Manitoba south to Georgia and Tennessee. Cultivated in England in 1755.

NANNYBERRY OR SHEEPBERRY *Viburnum lentago* L.

Native in North America from Quebec to Colorado, south to Georgia. Cultivated in England in 1761.

NEW JERSEY TEA *Ceanothus americanus* L.

Native in eastern North America from Quebec and Manitoba south to Florida and Alabama. Cultivated in England before 1713 by Bishop Compton.

OAK, BLACK *Quercus velutina* Lam.

Native from Maine to Nebraska, south to Florida and Texas.

OAK, BLACKJACK *Quercus marilandica* Muench.

Native from Pennsylvania to Nebraska, south to Florida and Texas.

OAK, CHESTNUT *Quercus prinus* L.

Native from Maine to Indiana, south to Georgia and Mississippi. Cultivated in England in 1730.

OAK, LIVE *Quercus virginiana* Miller

Native from Virginia to Texas and Oklahoma. Cultivated in England in 1739.

Oak, Southern Red   *Quercus falcata* Michx.
Native from New Jersey to Illinois, south to Florida and Texas. Cultivated in England in 1763.

Oak, Water   *Quercus nigra* L.
Native from Delaware to Kentucky, south to Florida and Texas. Cultivated in England in 1739.

Oak, Willow   *Quercus phellos* L.
Native from Long Island to Missouri, south to Florida and Texas. Confused at this time with Live Oak.

Olive, Russian, or Oleaster   *Elaeagnus angustifolia* L.
Native from Southern Europe to central Asia. Cultivated in England in 1633.

Pagoda tree, Japanese   *Sophora japonica* L.
Native in China and Korea. Cultivated in England in 1753.

Paper Mulberry, Common   *Broussonetia papyrifera* (L.) Vent.
Native in China and Japan. Cultivated in England in 1759, by Hugh, Duke of Northumberland. Female trees reported to be cultivated by 1768. Male trees said to have been introduced to New York by André Parmentier between 1824 and 1830.

Pawpaw   *Asimina triloba* (L.) Dunal
Native from New Jersey to Nebraska, south to Florida and Texas. Cultivated in England by Peter Collinson in 1736.

Pea-shrub, Siberian   *Caragana arborescens* Lam.
Native in Siberia and Manchuria. Cultivated in England in 1756.

Pecan, Mississippi Nut   *Carya illinoensis* K. Koch
Native from Indiana to Iowa, south to Alabama, Texas and Mexico. Introduced into England about 1766. Cultivated by William Prince of New York in 1772.

Persimmon   *Diospyros virginiana* L.
Native from New England to Kansas, south to Florida and

COLONIAL GARDENS 137

Texas. Cultivated in England in the time of Parkinson (1633).

PINE, VIRGINIA SCRUB *Pinus virginiana* Miller
Native from New Jersey and Ohio south to Georgia and Arkansas. Introduced into England before 1739.

PINE, WHITE, OR WEYMOUTH PINE *Pinus strobus* L.
Native from Newfoundland to Manitoba, south to Georgia and Tennessee. Cultivated in England by the Duchess of Beaufort in 1705.

PLUM, CHERRY, OR MYROBALAN PLUM *Prunus cerasifera* Ehrh.
Native in western Asia. Cultivated in England by 1600.

PLUM, DAMSON *Prunus insititia* L.
Native in western Asia and Europe. Cultivated since prehistoric times.

POISON OAK *Rhus toxicodendron* L. or *Rhus radicans* L.
Native over most of eastern North America. Cultivated in England in 1640.

POPLAR, EASTERN COTTONWOOD *Populus deltoides* Marshall
Native from Quebec to Manitoba, south to Florida and Texas. Cultivated in England before 1750.

POPLAR, LOMBARDY *Populus nigra* L. var. *italica*, Moench.
Native in Europe. Cultivated in France in 1749 and in England in 1758. Introduced by William Hamilton of Philadelphia in 1784.

POTENTILLA *Potentilla fruticosa* L.
Native throughout the northern hemisphere. Cultivated in England in 1700.

RED BAY *Persea borbonia* (L.) Sprengel
Native from Delaware south to Florida and Texas. Cultivated in England in 1739.

Rose, Cherokee — *Rosa laevigata* Michx.
Native in China. Introduced to the United States sometime before 1780.

Rose, Scotch — *Rosa spinosissima* L.
Native in Europe and western Asia. Cultivated before 1600.

Rose, Wild, or Swamp Rose — *Rosa palustris* Marshall
Native from Nova Scotia to Minnesota, south to Florida and Arkansas. Cultivated in England in 1726.

Shadblow, Service or Shad-bush
Amelanchier canadensis (L.) Medic.
Native in North America from Maine to New York, south to Georgia. Quite possibly cultivated, but the plant carrying this name in cultivation in Europe was probably *A. stolonifera* (see Mespilus, Snowy).

Silver bell, Carolina or Snowdrop Tree
Halesia carolina L.
Native from Virginia to Missouri, south to Florida and Texas. Cultivated in England by John Ellis in 1756 from seeds sent by Dr. Alexander Garden.

Sourwood — *Oxydendron arboreum* (L.) DC.
Native from Pennsylvania to Indiana south to Florida and Louisiana. Cultivated in England in 1752.

Spiraea, Hardhack — *Spiraea tomentosa* L.
Native from Prince Edward Island to Ontario, south to North Carolina. Cultivated in England in 1736 by Peter Collinson.

Stewartia — *Stewartia malachodendron* L.
Native from Virginia to Arkansas, south to Florida and Louisiana. Cultivated in England in 1743.

Stewartia, Mountain — *Stewartia ovata* (Cav.) Weatherby
Native from Virginia and Kentucky, south to Georgia and Alabama. Cultivated in England in 1785.

SUMAC, FRAGRANT, OR POLE-CAT BUSH *Rhus aromatica* Aiton
Native from Quebec to Kansas, south to Florida and Texas. Cultivated in England in 1772.

SWEET GALE *Myrica gale* L.
Native to Eurasia and North America. It has many folk uses in Europe.

THORN, GREAT-FRUITED OR LARGE-BERRIED
Crataegus punctatus Jacq.
Native from eastern Canada to Minnesota, south to Kentucky. Cultivated in Britain in 1746 by Archibald, Duke of Argyle.

TREFOIL, OR HOP-TREE *Ptelea trifoliata* L.
Native from Virginia south to Florida and Texas. Sent to England from Virginia by Rev. Banister in 1704.

UMBRELLA MAGNOLIA *Magnolia tripetala* L.
Native from Pennsylvania to Missouri, south to Georgia and Arkansas. Cultivated in England in 1752.

VIBURNUM, MAPLE LEAF *Viburnum acerifolium* L.
Native from Quebec to Minnesota, south to Georgia and Tennessee. Cultivated in England in 1736 by Peter Collinson.

WILLOW, VIRGINIA, OR SWEET SPIRE *Itea virginica* L.
Native from Pennsylvania to Missouri, south to Florida and Texas. Cultivated in Britain in 1744 by Archibald, Duke of Argyle.

WILLOW, WEEPING *Salix babylonica* L.
Native in China. Alleged to have been introduced to England by Alexander Pope about 1730.

WILLOW, YELLOW *Salix alba* L. var. *vitellina* (L.) Stokes
Native in Europe. Long cultivated for basket-making.

WINTERBERRY OR SWAMP RED-BERRY BUSH *Ilex verticillata*
(L.) Gray
Native from Newfoundland to Minnesota, south to Georgia and Tennessee. Cultivated in England in 1736 by Peter Collinson.

WINTERSWEET *Chimonanthus praecox* (L.) Link.
Native of China. Introduced into England by Benjamin Torin in 1771, or perhaps a little earlier.

WISTERIA, AMERICAN *Wisteria frutescens* (L.)
Poiret
Native from Virginia south to Florida and Alabama. Introduced in England in 1724 by Mark Catesby.

WITHEROD *Viburnum cassinoides* L.
Native from Newfoundland to Ontario, south to Alabama and Tennessee. Cultivated in England in 1761 by Mr. James Gordon.

YEW, ENGLISH YEW Probably *Taxus baccata* L.
Native in Europe and Western Asia. Cultivated since ancient times.

IX Fruits and Nuts, 1700 to 1776

BLACKBERRY *Rubus* sp.
Fruits of various species of *Rubus* were collected from plants growing spontaneously in hedge-rows. Blackberries were not cultivated until 1832.

CHESTNUT *Castanea dentata* (Marshall) Borkh.
Native from Maine to Minnesota, south to Florida and Mississippi.

CHESTNUT, FRENCH *Castanea sativa* Miller
Native in southern Europe, western Asia and North Africa. Cultivated by Thomas Jefferson in 1773.

CRAB APPLE *Malus angustifolia* (Aiton) Michx.
Native from Virginia to Florida and Mississippi. Introduced into cultivation in Britain in 1725.

CRANBERRY *Vaccinium macrocarpon* Aiton
Newfoundland to Minnesota, south to North Carolina and Arkansas. Fruit collected in the wild from early colonial times, but not cultivated until about 1820.

CURRANT, EUROPEAN BLACK *Ribes nigrum* L.
Native in Europe and northern and central Asia. Long cultivated.

MULBERRY, WHITE *Morus alba* L.
Native of China and Japan. Cultivated in America about 1660.

MULBERRY, RED *Morus rubra* L.
Native from Vermont to South Dakota, south to Florida and Texas. Cultivated in Britain in 1629.

OLIVE *Olea europaea* L.
Native in the Mediterranean region. Cultivated in South Carolina in 1775.

Horse chestnut, *Castanea equina cum flore*. From Gerarde, *Herball*.

APPENDIX

I

Examples of Authentic Colonial Gardens in New England

CONNECTICUT

Henry Witfield House (17th century), Guilford
Welles-Shipman House, Glastonbury
Isaac Stevens House, Wethersfield
Joseph Webb House, Wethersfield
Hatheway House, Suffield
Tappan Reeves Law Office, Litchfield
Noah Webster House, West Hartford

MAINE

Longfellow House, Portland

MASSACHUSETTS

Whipple House, Ipswich
Pliny Freeman Farm, Old Sturbridge Village, Sturbridge
Salem Towne House, Old Sturbridge Village, Sturbridge
Fitch House, Old Sturbridge Village, Sturbridge
Gardens at Plimouth Plantation, Plymouth
Mission House, Stockbridge
Coffin House, Nantucket

NEW HAMPSHIRE

Moffatt-Ladd House, Portsmouth

RHODE ISLAND

The Garden at Shakespear's Head, College Hill, off of Benefit Street, Providence
Governor Stephan Hopkins House, Benefit Street, College Hill, Providence
Smith's Castle, Cocumscussoc, U.S. 1, Wickford
Varnum Gardens, East Greenwich
'White Hall,' Middletown
Wanton-Lyman-Hazard House, Broadway Street, Newport

II

Authentic Plans for Colonial Garden Design

PEOPLE INTERESTED in colonial buildings and the grounds that surround them are excited to see that so many buildings and sites of this period are being carefully restored. Within recent years, restorers have used greater care in architectural restorations and have furnished buildings in an authentic manner.

Generally, this has not been true concerning the grounds. It is disappointing to see careful restorations ending with the four outer walls and no care given to making the grounds equally authentic. In one sense, this is betraying the viewer who expects a thorough and accurate representation of the period.

There are many carefully restored houses that have foundation plantings surrounding them. These are entirely wrong for they represent the period from about 1850 to after World War II and certainly not the colonial period. Within these plantings one finds Forsythia, not even introduced into England from the Orient until 1844; Japanese Yews, introduced into America from Japan in 1861; Pfitzer Juniper, introduced in 1901; Pachysandra, introduced in 1882; and *Spirea vanhouttei*, whose first documented date in America is 1866.

Certainly, the way in which plants are used around structures of the colonial period makes these buildings more authentic, real and alive.

It is the purpose of this article to present a documented list of authentic plants for the colonial period. Many lists exist but few are documented and it is possible to find errors and misinterpretations that have been perpetuated for over fifty years. Hopefully, this article will eliminate some of these errors.

In discussing the design aspects of the colonial era, we usually deal with the years 1620–1840 because design did not change drastically during this period. But in considering the plants, many nurseries and seed houses were established after the Revolutionary War, and many plants were imported; so we define the colonial period in its true, historical sense as 1620–1776, recognizing that there was a settlement in Jamestown, Virginia as early as 1607.

Plants in the Colonial Period

Although nurseries and seedhouses were few, research in this area reveals that there were many plants available. Many of them were brought over from Europe with the settlers, others were sent for, and there was a great deal of trading and exchange of slips, cuttings and seeds from person to person. The statement is often made by individuals and committees in charge of restoring old gardens and grounds that the kinds of plants available were limited. This is not true, as the following list shows. Perhaps there were fewer varieties and spectacular colors, but it was still easy to provide a 'splash' of color during the summer months.

The most common annuals during the colonial period were Four-O'Clocks in all the colors available today; Balsam, in red, white, purple, blush or pink, singles and doubles; the several Amaranthuses in the following list; Globe Amaranth, or Gomphrena, in purple or red, and white; Batchelor's Buttons in white, blue, purple and red; and Calendulas in yellow and orange.

Of the biennials, Sweet Williams were used extensively, in fact so much that they divided the shorter and narrower-leaved ones into a different common group called 'Sweet Johns.' Hollyhocks were plentiful, both singles and doubles, 'in several colors.' Believe it or not, two of the most popular garden flowers were Buttercups (Fair-Maids-of-France) and Dandelions. From these early gardens, these two flowers, among others, escaped from cultivation into the wild.

Three flowers used little today were very common during this period. Cowslips or Oxslips (Primroses) gave a great deal of color to the gardens of our early settlers and so did the Clove-Gilliflowers, Pinks, or Dianthus. Another common inhabitant of the garden was Feverfew or Featherfew. All of these flowers and others are mentioned in the list below.

Having listed a dozen or so of the most common flowers during the colonial era, how do these compare with what Richard Schermerhorn, Jr., considers the leaders of today?

PETUNIA   We have found no mention of this flower in the early garden books. Perhaps it was grown in the early gardens but the literature does not identify it as such. The name Petunia is a South American aboriginal name said to have been applied to tobacco. It is possible that Petunias are called tobacco or Nicotiana in some of the early books.

ZINNIA   These are listed quite frequently in the literature of the late 18th century but not in the early writings. It appears that they were just being introduced around the turn of the century (1800). Reds and yellows would be appropriate for that period.

MARIGOLD   The French Marigold (*Tagetes patula*) was used extensively quite early in the colonial period, but it appears that the African Marigold (*Tagetes erecta*) was not as common until around 1800 or later. The tiny, dwarf varieties that are so commonly used today would not be appropriate in an authentic restoration.

CHINA ASTER   Contrary to earlier lists, this plant was used during the colonial period, but it wasn't used as commonly as those flowers listed above. It seems that the most common varieties were single.

SWEET PEA   These were probably used throughout the colonial period, but we have not found a reference to them before the 1700's.

SNAPDRAGON   Although these do not appear to have been among the most common annuals, they were used very early and the most popular colors were red, white, purple, and variable.

LARKSPUR   These were used very early, but were not called Larkspur until late in the period. Earlier they were called Larks' Heels, or, correctly, Delphiniums.

MORNING GLORY   There seems to have been practically every color imaginable (red, white, purple, dark blue and striped) with the exception of today's popular "Heavenly Blue."

Bibliography

Andrews, Edward Deming and Andrews, Faith. *Shaker Herbs and Herbalists*. Berkshire Garden Center. Stockbridge, Mass. 1959.

Annual Report, Mount Vernon Ladies Assn. of the Union. Mt. Vernon, Virginia. 1964.

Bray, Mary Mathews. *My Grandmother's Garden and an Ancestral Orchard*. Richard G. Badger, Printer. Boston, Mass. 1931.

Cobbett, William. *The American Gardener*. C. Clement. London. 1821.

Downing, Andrew J. *A Treatise on the Theory and Practice of Landscape Gardening*. C. M. Saxon Co. N. Y. 1957. pp. 1–40.

Dudley, A. T. *The Moffatt-Ladd House*. Published by Colonial Dames in New Hampshire. pp. 14–16.

Earle, Alice Morse. *Old Time Gardens*. Macmillan Co. New York. 1928.

—*Sun-Dials and Roses of Yesterday*. Macmillan Co. New York. 1902.

Favretti, Rudy J. *Early New England Gardens, 1620–1840*. Old Sturbridge Village, Sturbridge, Mass. 1962.

—*New England Colonial Gardens*. Pequot Press. Stonington, Conn. 1964. pp. 4–5.

Fischer, Robert B. *The Mount Vernon Gardens*. The Mount Vernon Ladies Assn. of the Union. Mount Vernon, Virginia. 1960.

Hamlin, Talbot. *Greek Revival Architecture in America*. Dover Publications, Inc. New York. 1944. p. xv.

Hussey, Christopher. *English Gardens and Landscapes, 1700–1750.* Country Life. London. 1967.

Lawrence, John M. A. *A New System of Agriculture.* London. 1776.

Lockwood, Alice B. *Gardens of Colony and State.* Vol. I. Chas. Scribner & Sons. New York. 1931. pp. 20–21, 26–251.

Manks, Dorothy S. *How the American Nursery Trade Began.* In *Origins of American Horticulture, A Handbook,* Vol. XXIII, No. 3. Brooklyn Botanic Garden. N. Y. Autumn 1967. pp. 4–11.

M'Mahon, Bernard. *The American Gardeners Calendar.* Philadelphia. 1806. pp. 67–72.

Nichols, Frederick D. and Bear, James A. *Monticello.* Thomas Jefferson Memorial Association. 1967. pp. 53–64.

Rutman, Darrett B. *Husbandmen of Plymouth.* Beacon Press. Boston. 1967.

Schermerhorn, Richard, Jr. *Homes and Gardens of Old New York.* United States George Washington Bicentennial Commission. Washington, D.C. 1932. pp. 33–44.

Schurcliff, Arthur A. *Mount Vernon and Other Colonial Places of the South.* United States George Washington Bicentennial Commission. Washington, D.C. 1932. pp. 11–20.

—*Gardens of Old Salem and the New England Colonies.* United States George Washington Bicentennial Commission. Washington, D.C. 1932. pp. 45–53.

Slade, Daniel D. *The Evolution of Horticulture in New England.* Knickerbocker Press. New York. 1895. pp. 114–137.

Howells, John Mead. *The Architectural Heritage of the Merrimack.* Architectural Book Publishing Co., Inc. New York. 1941.

Stroud, Dorothy. *Capability Brown*. Country Life. London. 1957.

Wheelwright, Robert. *Gardens and Places of Colonial Philadelphia*. United States George Washington Bicentennial Commission.Washington, D.C. 1932. pp. 21–32.

Wilder, Marshall P. *The Horticulture of Boston and Vicinity*. Tolman & White, Printers. Boston. 1881.

RUDY J. FAVRETTI
*Associate Professor of
Landscape Design
University of Connecticut
Storrs, Connecticut*

III

Chronological Bibliography

The great value of a library is that it preserves the records of the work of one generation so that subsequent generations may benefit from them. Interest in the cultivated plants of the American colonies is not new. Records of the plants cultivated by the Indians were made by the first explorers of our continent. Travellers and residents throughout the colonial period recorded information on the plants that were under cultivation. The newspapers in the colonies carried advertisements of plants and seeds offered for sale. In recent years biographies of early horticulturists and botanists have added much to our knowledge.

The following list of book titles does not pretend to be complete. Indeed, many important titles, published in the nineteenth and early twentieth centuries, have been omitted. However, in conjunction with the lists of titles given in the preceding articles, the inquiring reader can make a beginning on the study of the cultivated plants of the colonial period.

1588   Harriot, Thomas. *A Briefe and True Report of the New Found Land of Virginia* . . (London.) I. Wechel. Frankfort-am-Main. 1590.

1608 Smith, John. *A True Relation of such Occurance and Accidents of Noate as hath hapned in Virginia* . . J. Tappe. London.

1611 Lascarbot, Marc. *Histoire de la Nouvelle-France* . . , 2nd. ed. Paris.

1612 Smith, John. *A Map of Virginia, with a Description* . . J. Barnes. Oxford.

1614 —*A Description of New England* . . H. Lownes. London.

1624 —*General Historie of Virginia, New England, and the Summer Isles*. I.D. and I.H. London. 1626, 1632.

1630 Higginson, Francis. *New England's Plantation*. T.C. and R.C. for M. Sparke. London.

1634 Wood, William. *New England's Prospect*, 2nd. ed. Tho. Cotes. London. 1635.

1636 Sagard-Theodat, Gabriel. *Histoire du Canada*. Paris.

1637 Morton, Thomas. *New English Canaan*. Jacob Frederick Stam. Amsterdam.

1650 Williams, Edward. *Virginia* . . , 2nd ed. T.H. for J. Stephenson. London.

1654 Johnson, Edward. *A History of New England* . . (*Wonder Working Providence of Sions Savior in New England*). Nath. Brooke. London. 1653.

1655 Hartlib, Samuel. *The Reformed Virginia Silkworm* . . G. Calvert. London.

1656 Tradescant, John, Jr. *Museum Tradescantianum* . . John Grismond. London.

1670 Denton, Daniel. *A Briefe Description of New York* .. John Hancock. London.

1672 Josselyn, John. *New England's Rarities Discovered* .. Giles Widdowes. London.

1674 —*An Account of Two Voyages to New England* .. Giles Widdowes. London.

1682 Ash, Thomas. *Carolina, or a Description of the Present State of that Country*. London.

1682 Wilson, Samuel. *An Account of the Province of Carolina* .. G. Larkin for F. Smith. London.

1683 Penn, William. *Letter from William Penn to the Committee of the Free Society of Traders*. Andrew Sowle. London.

1703 La Hontan, Armand Louis, Baron de Norveaux. *New Voyages to North America* .., English trans. H. Bonwicke, T. Goodwin, M. Wotton & B. Tooke. London.

1709 Lawson, John. *A New Voyage to Carolina* .. London.

1710 Anon. *The Husbandman's Guide*, 2nd ed. John Allen for Eleazor Phillips. Boston, Mass. 1712.

1714 Lawson, John. *The History of Carolina* .. W. Taylor and F. Baker. London.

1724 Jones, Hugh. *The Present State of Virginia*. J. Clarke. London.

1731–43 Catesby, Mark. *Natural History of Carolina, Florida, and the Bahama Islands*. The Author. London. 2nd ed., 1754; 3rd ed., 1771.

1737 Brickell, John. *The Natural History of North Carolina* .. J. Carson. Dublin.

1742 Colden, Cadwallader. *Plantae Coldenhamiae*. Uppsala.

1751 Bartram, John. *Observations* .. J. Whiston and B. White. London.

1758 Le Page du Pratz. *Histoire de la Louisiane* .., 3 vols. De-Bure. Paris. (English ed. in 2 vols. T. Becket and P. A. DeHondt. London. 1763.)

1758 Pullein, Samuel. *The Culture of Silk: or an Essay for the Use of the American Colonies*. A. Miller. London.

1759 Acrelius, Israel. *Description of the Former and Present State of New Sweden*. Harberg & Hesselberg. Stockholm. (English trans. in *Memoirs of the Pennsylvania Historical Society*. Philadelphia. 1874.)

1760–61 Jefferys, Thomas. *The Natural and Civil History of the French Dominions*. London.

1763 Catesby, Mark. *Hortus Britanico-Americanus* .. W. Richardson and S. Clark. London.

1765 Smith, Samuel. *The History of the Colony of Nova-Caesaria, or New Jersey*. J. Parker. Burlington, N.J.

1766 Eliot, Jared. *Essays upon Field-Husbandry in New England* .. Edes and Gill. Boston. ('The Foregoing essays were first printed in New London and New York ..' between 1748 and 1759.)

1770–71 Kalm, Pehr. *Travels into North America* .., trans. from the Swedish ed. of 1753–61. Warrington. London.

1775 Mallat, Robert X. [?] *American Husbandry*, 2 vols. Bew. London.

1778 Carver, Jonathan. *Travels Through the Interior Parts of North America* .. London.

1782 Crèvecoeur, Michel Guillaume St. John de (J. Hector St. John, pseud.). *Letters from an American Farmer* . . Thomas Davies and Luckyer Davis. London.

1785 Cutler, Manasseh. *An Account of some of the Vegetable Productions Naturally Growing in this Part of America, Botanically Arranged.* Memoirs of the American Academy . . I, 396–493.

1785 Marshall, Humphrey. *Arbustrum Americanum: The American Grove* . . J. Crukshank. Philadelphia.

1784– Belknap, Jeremy. *History of New Hampshire.* 'Forest
92 Trees and other Vegetable Productions,' III, 96–127. Robert Aitken. Philadelphia.

1787 Squibb, Robert. *The Gardener's Calendar for the State of North Carolina, South Carolina, and Georgia.* Charleston.

1789 Anburey, Thomas. *Travels Through the Interior Parts of America,* 2 vols. William Lane. London.

1790 Deane, Samuel. *The New England Farmer; or Georgical Dictionary* . . Isaiah Thomas. Worcester, Boston.

1791 Bartram, William. *Travels through Carolina, Georgia, Florida* . . James and Johnson. Philadelphia.

1792 Eddis, William. *Letters from America* . . The Author. London.

1792 Imray. *Description of the Western Territory of North America.* London.

1794 Williams, Samuel. *Natural and Civil History of Vermont.* 'Forest Trees, Esculent and Medicinal Vegetables,' pp. 67–71. Isaiah Thomas and David Carlisle. Walpole, N. H.

1796 Dabney, John. *An Address to Farmers . . To which is added an appendix containing the most approved methods for the management and improvement of tillage.* J. Dabney. Salem, Mass.

1799 Marshall, Charles. *An Introduction to the Knowledge and Practice of Gardening . .*, 1st American ed. from the 2nd London ed. J. Nancrede. Boston.

* * * * * * * *

1849 Darlington, William. *Memorials of John Bartram and Humphrey Marshall . .* Lindsay and Blakiston. Philadelphia.

1879 Pickering, C. *Chronological History of Plants . .* Boston.

1895 Slade, D.D. *The Evolution of Horticulture in New England.* Putnam's Sons. New York, London.

1927 Woodward, C.R. *The Development of Agriculture in New Jersey, 1640–1880.* N.J. Agr. Expt. Sta. Bull. 451.

1933 Gray, L.C. *History of Agriculture in the Southern United States to 1860.* The Carnegie Institution of Washington. Washington.

1933 Hedrick, U.P. *A History of Agriculture in New York.* New York State Agr. Soc. Albany, N.Y.

1958 Bartram, W., ed. Francis Harper. *Travells.* Yale University Press. New Haven.

1961 Frick, G.F. and Stearns, R.P. *Mark Catesby, The Colonial Audubon.* Univ. of Illinois. Urbana, Ill.

1963 Berkeley, E. and Berkeley, D.C. *John Clayton, Pioneer of American Botany.* Univ. of North Carolina. Chapel Hill, N.C.

1964 Allen, M. *The Tradescants, Their Plants, Gardens, and Museum, 1570–1662*. Michael Joseph. London.

1969 Berkeley, E. and Berkeley, D.C. *Dr. Alexander Garden of Charles Town*. Univ. of North Carolina. Chapel Hill, N.C.

Bibliography

Abercrombie, John. *The Gardener's Daily Assistant*. London. 1786.

'American Garden Milestones,' *Flower Grower Magazine*. Vol. XLVI, No. 12. New York. Dec. 1959. p. 24.

Bailey, Liberty Hyde. *The Standard Cyclopedia of American Horticulture*. Vols. I, II, III. The Macmillan Co. New York. 1933.

Bailey, Liberty Hyde and Bailey, Ethel Zoe. *Hortus Second*. The Macmillan Co. New York. 1947.

Betts, Edwin Morris. *Thomas Jefferson's Garden Book*. The American Philosophical Society. Memoirs. Vol. XXII. Philadelphia. 1944.

Bourne, H. *The Florist's Manual*. Monroe and Francis. Boston. 1833.

Clapham, A. R., Tuton, T. G., and Warburg, E. F. *Flora of the British Isles*. Cambridge University Press. Cambridge. 1952.

Dodoens, R. *A Niewe Herball*. H. Lyte, trans. Gerard Dewes. London. 1578.

Emerson, G. B. *Trees and Shrubs of Massachusetts*. Little, Brown and Co. Boston. 1846.

Favretti, Rudy J. *Early New England Gardens, 1620–1840*. Old Sturbridge Village. Sturbridge, Mass. 1962.

—*New England Colonial Gardens*. Pequot Press. Stonington, Conn. 1964.

Fisher, Robert B. *The Mount Vernon Gardens*. The Mount Vernon Ladies' Association. Mount Vernon, Va. 1960.

Fogg, John M. *Common Weeds from Europe*. Published in *Origins of American Horticulture, A Handbook*. Vol. xxiii, No. 3. Brooklyn Botanic Garden. New York. Autumn, 1967.

Gerarde, John. *Herball (Or Generall Historie of Plantes)*. John Norton. London. 1597.

Hedrick, U. P. *A History of Horticulture in America to 1860*. Oxford University Press. New York. 1950.

Hedrick, U. P. et al. *The Cherries of New York*. Ann. Rep't. N. Y. Agr. Expt. Sta. No. 22, Vol. ii, Pt. ii. J. B. Lyon Co. Albany, N. Y. 1915.

—*The Grapes of New York*. Ann. Rep't. N. Y. Agr. Expt. Sta. No. 15, Vol iii, Pt. ii. J. B. Lyon Co. Albany, N. Y. 1908.

—*The Peaches of New York*. Ann. Rep't. N. Y. Agr. Expt. Sta. No. 24, Vol. ii, Pt. ii. J. B. Lyon Co. Albany, N. Y. 1917.

—*The Pears of New York*. Ann. Rep't. N. Y. Agr. Expt. Sta. No. 29, Vol. ii, Pt. ii. J. B. Lyon Co. Albany, N. Y. 1921.

—*The Plums of New York*. Ann. Rep't. N. Y. Agr. Expt. Sta. No. 18, Vol. iii, Pt. ii. J. B. Lyon Co. Albany, N. Y. 1911.

—*The Small Fruits of New York*. Ann. Rep't. N. Y. Agr. Expt. Sta. No. 31, Pt. ii. J. B. Lyon Co. Albany, N. Y. 1925.

Hedrick, U. P., ed. *Sturtevant's Notes on Edible Plants*. Ann. Rep't. N. Y. Agr. Expt. Sta. No. 27, Vol. II, Pt. II. J. B. Lyon Co. Albany, N. Y. 1919.

Hughes, William. *The Flower Garden and Compleat Vinyard*, 3rd ed. London. 1683.

Josselyn, John. *New England Rarities*. London. 1673.

Kalm, Peter. *Travels in North America, The America of 1750*. Vols. I, II. Dover Publications. New York. 1964.

Kammerer, E. L. *What Woody Plants Were Used in American Colonial Gardens*. Morton Arboretum Bulletin, Lisle, Ill. Vol. XX, No. 2. Feb. 1947.

Lawson, William. *The Country Housewife's Garden*. London. 1617.

Manks, Dorothy S. *How the American Nursery Trade Began*. Published in *Origins of American Horticulture, A Handbook*. Vol. XXIII, No. 3. Brooklyn Botanic Garden. New York. Autumn 1967. p. 4.

—*Early American Nurserymen and Seedsmen*. Published in *Origins of American Horticulture, A Handbook*. Vol. XXIII, No. 3. Brooklyn Botanic Garden. New York.
Autumn 1967. p. 75.

Miller, Philip. *The Gardener's Dictionary*, 7th ed. London. 1759.

Miller, Philip. (Thomas Martyn, ed.) *The Gardener's Dictionary*. London. 1797–1804.

Parkinson, John. *Paradisi in sole, Paradisus Terrestris*. London. 1629.

—*Theatrum botanicum* . . . London. 1640.

Platt, Sir Hugh (Knight). *The Garden of Eden*, 5th ed. London. 1659.

Rea, John (Gent.) *Flora: Sev de florum cultura*. London. 1665.

Richardson, Josiah. *The New England Farrier and Family Physician*. Exeter, N.H. 1828. pp. 56, 379.

Rockwell, Fred F. and Grayson, Esther C. *The Complete Book of Annuals*. American Garden Guild and Doubleday and Co., Inc. Garden City, New York. 1955. p. 181.

Sargent, C. S. *Extracts from General Washington's Diary Relating to Trees and Plants* (Handwritten Manuscript). Boston Athenaeum.

Slade, Daniel P. *The Evolution of Horticulture in New England*. Knickerbocker Press. New York. 1895.

Sturtevant. See Hedrick, U. P.

Taylor, Raymond L. *Plants of Colonial Days*. Colonial Williamsburg. 1968.

Thompson, Homer C. *Vegetable Crops*, 4th ed. McGraw-Hill Book Co., Inc. New York. 1949.

Wilder, Marshall P. *The Horticulture of Boston and Vicinity*. Tolman and White. Boston, Mass. 1881.

Williamsburg: *Authentic Plant Materials for Gardens of Colonial Williamsburg*. Williamsburg Garden Symposium Mimeograph. Williamsburg, Va.

Worcester County Horticultural Society: *List and Order Sheet of Scions for Grafting*. Worcester County Horticultural Society, 30 Elm Street, Worcester, Mass.

Wyman, Donald. *Introductory Dates of Familiar Trees, Shrubs and Vines. Origins of American Horticulture, A Handbook*. Vol. XXIII, No. 3. Brooklyn Botanic Garden. New York. Autumn 1967. p. 87.

—*Shrubs and Vines for American Gardens*. The Macmillan Co. New York. 1949.

—*Trees for American Gardens*. The Macmillan Co. New York. 1951.

Colonial Gardens is printed in an edition of 4,000 at the press of David R. Godine. The photographs have been printed by The Meriden Gravure Company. The type, Baskerville, has been composed by Salisbury Printers and has been printed on Mohawk Superfine paper.